Fisher in the West

An experience of Hebridean angling

by EDDIE YOUNG

Published, designed and printed by Stornoway Gazette Ltd., 10 Francis Street, Stornoway, Isle of Lewis. Telephone 01851-702687.

© Stornoway Gazette Ltd 1994

Cover photo: Ian Scarr-Hall. Courtesy of Borve Lodge Estate.

ISBN 0-903960-07-9

ABOUT THE AUTHOR

WHEN Eddie Young angled for perch in ponds near his home in Lanarkshire prior to graduating to fishing the Upper Clyde and Tweed at the age of twelve, he was preparing the way for a lifetime dedicated to the spare-time pursuit of the noble art. In these days he used all manner of (legal) techniques and settled early on fly-fishing with both dry and wet flies. He caught trout (on diminutive Clyde "flees") 7,000 feet up in the hills in India during war service with the Queen's Own Cameron Highlanders as well as large carp from the moat of a mediaeval Japanese castle where he was stationed after the war.

On his arrival in Lewis in 1968 as Rector of The Nicolson Institute he set himself two tasks, both of which he carried through with distinction. His first task was to carry on the great tradition of a great school and he dedicated the final 21 years of a distinguished teaching career to that task with supreme professionalism. His second task was to re-learn his angling in a totally different environment and his conversion to loch fishing was completed after a two-year settling-in period. Needless to say he never forgot his skills on the river.

He is a good fishing companion and a meticulous fisher — always well prepared and observant — and his fishing diaries record his triumphs and disappointments over the years as well as not a few escapades. He revived his skills as a fly-dresser and true to his calling taught hundreds of young lads (and lasses) and not-so-young colleagues and fellow anglers to dress their own flies in his informal school activity classes and adult evening sessions.

When retirement brought him a welcome respite from responsibility he did not have to look far to fill his time and he added angling journalism to his already extensive angling repertoire. His regular features in the local press and national angling journals are scholarly, informative, colloquial and humorous and are a literary focal point for locals as well as many "from away" judging by his mailbag.

When he was finally persuaded to collect some of his writings in a book which would interest local and visiting anglers he set about the task with customary thoroughness. The book is a superb insight into Eddie Young's "ways with the angle" as well as a fitting companion on the angler's bookshelf to "Trout Fishing in Lewis" by the late Norman Macleod which Eddie has jointly edited in its two reprint editions.

To the people of the Western Isles

with gratitude for educating me in the ways of fish and of friendship.

PREFACE

IT IS customary for the angling writer to excuse yet another book on fishing. My reasons, not excuses, are twofold and simple: first, to give some idea to visitors, potential visitors and recent arrivals of the delights of living in such a welcoming community and of fishing in such wild and beautiful places; second, to be unashamedly self-indulgent in reliving the deep and lasting experience of over twenty-five years of such fishing and such friends. The two reasons are not unconnected.

In addition, as one of my fishing friends put it to me, with the generosity of spirit and the supreme tactlessness which only the dedicated fisher can achieve: "I think you ought to consider writing a book about fishing here so that you can leave something behind you when you are gone!"

What follows should give the reader some flavour of fishing here; incidentally and, I hope, painlessly passing on advice based on the experience of many others, past and present, so that newcomers and visitors to the islands can enjoy more fully the excitements and the joys of angling in the Outer Hebrides. Indeed there are many who have come here on holiday, then wisely decided to retire here (often early) to live in what is a constantly stimulating and vibrant community of remarkable people. The fishing is a bonus.

ACKNOWLEDGEMENTS

THIS book is based on articles which have appeared over the years in the internationally famous angling magazine, *Trout & Salmon* and which appear here, with some modifications, through the courtesy of its Editor, Sandy Leventon. Some have appeared in the *Eilean an Fraoich* (Island of Heather) *Annual* published by the *Stornoway Gazette*, which has a world-wide circulation both among exiled Gaels and our regular visitors to the Western Isles. Some additional material has come from my Angling Lines column in the Gazette. I am grateful to the Editor for his kindness in allowing me to draw on these sources. The line drawings are by my younger daughter, Alison —not a fisher but immensely tolerant of her father's obsession. David Maclennan has given sound advice and ensured that the natural history background caontains few howlers. To both my thanks for their willing help.

Angus Morrison, Business Manager of *The Stornoway Gazette* first suggested I write this book and kept at me until I did. Neil MacRitchie, Caseroom Foreman, has been a constant and patient adviser on the mysteries of his craft. It is no accident that both are very knowledgeable anglers.

I am especially indebted to Roddy John Macleod, my co-editor of *"Trout Fishing In Lewis"* (1993), for subjecting the text to the same close scrutiny he used to give to all I wrote when we were professional colleagues, for his constant support and for his valuable suggestions. The remaining errors are all mine.

Finally, I wish to record my deep appreciation of the kindness of all my fishing friends throughout these islands, of the members of the close-season fly-tying group over many years, and of those met by the loch side who have instructed, corrected, inspired and encouraged me in my fishing, with that special blend of genuine concern and cheerful insult which are the marks of true friendship in these parts. When you receive it, you know you have arrived.

INTRODUCTION

THE word "Hebrides" (etymology uncertain) contains for English speakers acquainted with their own literature a powerful emotional association with remoteness and mystery. Milton uses it in "Lycidas":
>". . . where'er thy bones are hurled,
>Whether beyond the stormy Hebrides..."

and Wordsworth in "The Solitary Reaper":
>"A voice so thrilling ne'er was heard
>In springtime from the cuckoo-bird,
>Breaking the silence of the seas
>Among the farthest Hebrides."

Gaelic speakers feel it differently, but no less intensely, as in the anonymous "Canadian Boat Song" of eighteenth century exiles:
>"From the lone sheiling of the misty island
>Mountains divide us , and waste of seas —
>Yet still the blood is strong, the heart is Highland,
>And we in dreams behold the Hebrides."

The Western Isles, the Outer Hebrides, the most westerly part of the United Kingdom, are unique. There is no other word for them. This uniqueness lies in their climate, their topography, their wild life and, above all, their people. To appreciate these fully, it is necessary to live here over a long period of time and thus become, stage by stage, more deeply immersed into their uniqueness. Fortunately for the visiting angler many of these joys are immediate, obvious and accessible. I hope that the following will give the incoming angler a helpful background of knowledge which may lead to a deeper understanding and appreciation of this uniqueness — and perhaps help to catch more fish!

Climate

The climate, like that of the rest of the United Kingdom, is maritime, lying between the wet air of the Atlantic and the drier air of continental Europe. It is better described as highly oceanic, affecting the distribution of many floral species often found at much lower altitudes in the Islands than they are on the peaks of the Mainland — a phenomenon known as oceanicity. In the Western Isles we are on the extreme climatic frontier, and so life, as on frontiers everywhere, can be full of incident, with changes of weather even more frequent than on the mainland, and highly variable within the islands themselves — from west to east and according to altitude.

It can be wet: the average rainfall for Stornoway, the capital, is around 43 inches. Winds can be strong as fronts move rapidly in from the west, and the angler must be well protected from horizontal rain, but such depressions are often of short duration. This alternation of wind and rain on the one hand and calm and sun on the other is part of the fascination of a Hebridean day. Surprisingly often, in summer, a continental anti-cyclone envelops the islands, bringing hot sun and calm airs from the east. The wildness and wet give way to a paradisal landscape of great beauty, and the fisher becomes reintroduced to his or her family and joins them in sunbathing on our marvellously underpopulated beaches.

But beware of the sun. Because of the clarity of the unpolluted air, sunburn can strike the unwary, and those fishing from a boat on a loch on such a day may have to decorate their faces with sun-blocker like Australian cricketers — though with, perhaps, more restraint.

Geology

This affects the angler indirectly. The underlying rocks are predominantly Lewisian gneiss, one of the oldest rocks in the world, dating back 3000 million years, and now often exposed through the erosion of younger rock above them. The area was heavily glaciated by successive ice ages, depositing glacial till and causing morainic drift over the impervious gneiss, creating a landscape of peat moor and generally acidic soil.

The lochs, except for those on the west coast where blown calcareous sand from the beaches has sweetened them, are also on the acid side of neutral, though this does not prevent many lochs producing trout of very high quality through the influence of other physical factors. Because of the blanket of peat (itself the product of the impervious sub-soil and a wet, cold climate which arrests the decay of vegetation) many lochs have peat-stained water, but in most the water is perfectly clear because they lie either on the clean bed-rock or on the washed gravels of the last departing ice-sheet. The angler can thus expect lochs where the fish can see the flies easily — and their bogus nature — which is one more reason to fish smaller than you might expect.

There are plenty of lochs to choose from. In "The Hebrides, A Natural History" by J M Boyd and I L Boyd (see Bibliography) the authors draw attention to the startling statistic that we have only 1.3% of the land area of the UK but 15% of the standing water. Or, as one non-academic observer put it: "Two thirds of the land surface is water!"

Safety

"A punishing and highly changeable climate" say Boyd and Boyd, referring to the whole year, not just the angler's summer. Combine this with the often featureless nature of the moorland, especially in Lewis, and the necessity for wearing good waterproof (preferably breathable) clothing, stout well-cleated wellingtons, and carrying map, compass and whistle becomes obvious. Make sure you know how to use a compass and read a map. It is very easy to become lost in some parts, even for residents. Take all the usual precautions.

Boats are not for standing up in, especially on a windswept loch. You are strongly advised to wear a buoyancy aid or lifejacket. The modern ones do not restrict your movements and may save your life. Often yours may be the only boat on a loch and therefore you cannot rely on help from others. Check boat equipment carefully and carry spares.

The fish

Brown trout, sea trout and salmon with the very occasional arctic charr (salvelinus alpinus) are the quarry. There are no so-called coarse fish but lots and lots of eels! Salmon anglers don't need two-handed rods and large flies, necessary on some mainland salmon rivers. A single-handed rod of AFTM 6 to 8 of between 10 and 11 feet long is more than adequate, and at the end of a long day of casting your arm muscles will not be strained. For our brown trout a rod of around 10 feet, AFTM 5-6, is ideal.

Fitness

We may not often think about fitness in connection with fishing, but it should be seriously considered before the beginning of any new season anywhere so that we can get the best out of it, and certainly before any angling holiday here. Walking the moor, especially after rain, is altogether different from walking on paths and tracks. It can be a strength-sapping experience even for the conventionally fit. The terrain and climate are something like the Falkland Islands, and though you would never load yourself with the equipment of a Royal Marine Commando yomping to Port Stanley, even a short walk with a light load can have the unprepared puffing badly.

It makes sense to walk off the fat of winter and prepare the muscles for more strenuous work. Your holiday will be all the more pleasurable for this kind of preparation, and you will feel enormously fit at the end of it. Don't try to cram too much into a short time: take a long holiday!

Wildlife

Birds of the moorland and the shore abound. In spring the moor can be a very noisy place indeed, and the angler on the loch can have many distractions . Golden eagles are not uncommon and lead to many a missed take. Divers, blackthroated and red-throated, fly overhead or float at a discreet distance; sandpipers, golden plovers, lapwings and wrens haunt the lochside. The heron, a much better fisher than any of us, reminds us of the necessity of wearing drab clothing and of moving slowly and quietly when bank fishing.

Especially early and late the angler will see many deer on the hill or by the loch, and the mountain hare is making a comeback after years of scarcity. It is astonishingly easy to trip over an otter in the dark!

The quality of fishing in these wild places lies in much more than the fish. May you have tight lines — and many distractions.

The fishing diary

Anglers know the value of keeping a record of each day's fishing for the obvious practical reasons of recording not only catches (or the lack of them) but also the weather conditions, time of year, type of water, flies used etc which may have affected the chances of success on a particular day. The wise angler constantly refers to past entries in order to learn more about our craft and, simply, to catch more and better fish.

But there are other reasons. From my youth I have intermittently kept a fishing diary, but it is a measure of the fascination of fishing here that I have now full records of my fishing over the past 25 years without a single blank. The diaries record much more than the vital statistics outlined above. During the close season they bring back the joys and the disappointments of an active angling life, something like Wordsworth's "emotion recollected in tranquillity", reminding the diarist of the sheer fun and excitement of past days and stimulating him, if such were necessary, in the anticipation of yet another season's wandering among our wild and beautiful landscape.

What follows is linked by the diaries. If some of what is written seems over-personal, that is the nature of the genre, but it is all firmly based on experience and is, at least as far as a fisherman can manage, substantially true!

Chapter 1

ONE of my earliest Hebridean diary entries dates from the first few weeks here. Everyone in the world seems to know about Barra because of Compton Mackenzie's "Whisky Galore" and the much appreciated repeated showings of the film made from it on television. Barra is, of course, a far more complex and fascinating island than the book or film indicates, but the story of the "Politician" has an irresistible appeal to all of us who like the idea of cocking a snook at authority, no matter how respectable we like to be thought in public.

It was my good luck to meet thus early someone, then a much respected member of the community, who in his youth had direct experience of that famous incident in modern Hebridean folklore. As a young joiner in wartime he and a colleague were sent to Barra to complete a contract. Before leaving Stornoway they had with great good fortune acquired a bottle of whisky, at that time something rare and precious, which they took with them to Barra "purely for medicinal purposes", as I was assured. Strangers in a hitherto strange island they were made warmly welcome in the traditional Barra manner especially by an old crofter who helped them in many little ways , finally inviting them to a ceilidh in his house one evening.

They had a serious debate about making a contribution to the evening's enjoyment, finally coming, after much soul-searching to a firm moral decision to contribute their carefully hoarded bottle. Their host's house resounded with music and laughter as they entered through the wartime black-out and stood blinking in the warmth and light of a good-going party, holding their bottle out as their gift, to be met with roars of helpless mirth. As my friend put it: "The whole room was wall-papered with crates of the stuff".

Many years later another friend was standing on the Cockle Strand, Barra's unique airport where the planes land on the beach at low tide, looking out towards Eriskay and the place where the "Politician" had been wrecked. Beside him stood a well-known Barra priest. To make conversation, my friend remarked, "I hear the divers brought up a few more bottles from the wreck last week. After such a long immersion in sea water I suppose the whisky wouldn't be worth drinking."

The priest, still with his eyes fixed on Eriskay, remarked, "Wasn't bad."

The most southerly of our main islands, Barra has its own special and very attractive quality of life. It is not famous for its fishing, like its more northerly neighbours, South Uist, Benbecula and North Uist, but it has one very good loch and some interesting minor ones. As I have suggested,Barra humour is worth experiencing even if you are at the receiving end (reassuringly,it is always gentle) and a visit to this very beautiful island, perfect for a family holiday, will give you the best possible introduction in miniature to the rest of the Western Isles.

Charm

"We had a charming day," said a rather gushing lady visitor as she tried to express her delight at spending a summer's day here in the Outer Hebrides. I was a bit taken aback at her use of the word, not being in the habit of using it for anything, but it made me think.

"Charm" was once a word of power, associated with magic and necromancy. Nowadays it has rather old-fashioned, somewhat twee connotations. Occasional visitors to these islands tend to throw it about rather loosely, perhaps understandably overcome by the experience of glorious days spent on sunspeckled machair lochs with the curlews calling and the distant hills beginning to purple with the heather bloom. These have "charm" all right, but even such beautiful images still restrict the word.

"Charm" in a Hebridean context suggests something richer, more varied, more deeply satisfying than simply the beauty of landscape and wildlife. Here it suggests the unpredictability of a fishing day; the sudden shifts of weather and light; the Hebridean sense of humour — itself full of delicate nuances — expressing itself in subtly timed and carefully precise utterance, the whole experience leading to a heightening of one's perceptions in the sheer delight at being alive in such surroundings and among such people. And such fish.

I used to be lucky enough to visit, as part of my work, the islands south of Lewis every late April or early May. These included Harris (not geographically an island but still very much the Isle of Harris in the eyes of its people), North Uist, Benbecula, South Uist and Barra. I found that, however busy each day could be, there was always an hour or two to try out a new loch or revisit an old, for in the Western Isles you work just as hard as anywhere else — but you recover more quickly.

A four-piece glass-fibre rod, rated 6-7 travelled with me, safe in its 2½ feet of plastic piping. A supermarket plastic bag contained my wellies, and into my fishing bag I crammed my tackle, an old shirt and pullover, and a pair of even older moleskins. Loganair, a truly civilised airline, was infinitely helpful and patiently understanding on the subject of anglers' impedimenta.

I could change from the conspicuously respectable to the inconspicuously disreputable in a matter of minutes, though, unlike Superman, I didn't use telephone boxes. I like to think, however, that my personality changed just as rapidly, and certainly for the better.

I wore my best fishing jacket for travelling. I long ago gave up buying raincoats and overcoats. A good fishing jacket (not waxed cotton) can be worn with assurance in both polite and impolite society, eventually to be retired to do its proper job when its scruffiness has matured to the point of improving one's camouflage at the loch-side.

My companion on these visits was Donald, a university academic who lectured on Scottish History and nurtured a passion for hill-walking and archaeology. Like Sir Walter Scott he was "not a fisher, but a friend of fishers" and would happily gillie for me in a variety of boats with a skill that could not have been wholly learned. More likely it was inherited from a long line of Border ancestors: fishers, poachers, rievers and probably worse. If I were bank-fishing Donald would remain until the first trout was landed, such was his faith in me. Then, feeling his duty done, he would disappear in the direction of the nearest tumulus, souterrain or stone circle.

Once on Barra, that most beautiful of islands, we had the afternoon off. We decided that I should fish Loch an Duin in the north of the island while Donald went off into the hills to explore a prehistoric site. We had no transport, but the ever-obliging Castlebay Post Office provided us with bicycles. Unfortunately the summer stock had not yet arrived, and we had to make do with children's machines still awaiting their annual servicing.

Clad in our oldest clothes and after some frantic initial wobbling we had no great difficulty in making our bandy-legged way along seven miles of the west cost and its glorious beaches, after which I spent a pleasant hour fishing for the small but very game trout in this attractive loch. Invicta, Black Pennell and Cinnamon and Gold on sizes 12 and 14 on 3lb nylon had been recommended by Reg Allan, at that time one of Barra's regional councillors. He once showed me the trick of sending his dog ahead to beat the bushes and create a localised fall of flies. It worked, if I may use the word, like a charm. I had no dog that day, but the fly patterns and sizes were entirely satisfactory.

The weather then began to worsen, with a near gale and squalls of rain blowing up from the south. Donald returned from the hill, and we foolishly decided to complete the circuit of Barra by battling down the east-coast road, head-on at times to the wind, finally with only (only?) the great bulk of Heaval to overcome. Several false crests later and with the red mist of what should have been our first coronaries before our eyes , we arrived at the highest point of the road and saw, spread before us, the magnificent sight of Castlebay harbour and Kismul's Castle. No more strained-back pedalling; no more puff and push. It would be an exhilarating run downhill with that spectacular view before and below us.

From the top, the road looped and twisted down like the last stages of the old Monte Carlo rally or, as we soon found out, the Cresta Run without the snow. Donald took the lead. Soon a cry of despair whipped back along his slipstream: "My brakes have burst!" Fortunately he was wearing his climbing boots, which he managed to use as an auxiliary braking system to keep him from taking off at each bend, but the commando soles were paper thin when we reached the bottom. My own problem was staying on the road throughout alternate convulsions of stark terror and helpless hilarity. Finally, surprised to be still alive , we stumbled — thoroughly shaken and certainly stirred —into that most hospitable of hotels, the Craigard, and not so much drank our pints of shandy as absorbed them until at last the trembling stopped. As we slowly recovered we were at least reassured that no one could possibly have recognised such respectable visitors in the two tatterdemalions who had been insane enough to go cycling, on children's bicycles, in such weather. The next day, clad once more in pin-striped respectability, we went on board the little ferry-boat, the "Ferry Likely" — named according to local tradition as the standard reply to the tourist's enquiry as to whether she would sail that day — which was to take us to South Uist. As we left the jetty the ferryman leaned over to me confidentially and said, with carefully modulated concern, "And did you enjoy your cycle run, Mr Young?" There are no secrets on Barra.

The best loch on Barra, Loch Tangusdale (Loch St Clair, on the OS map), provides a different class of fish from Loch an Duin. That is a machair loch, sweetened by the calcareous sand blown in from the dunes between it and the sea, and given additional feeding from the varied products of the two crofts beside it, especially the (happily filtered) contribution made by some fine cattle beasts. In consequence it grows magnificent trout: beautifully marked, red-fleshed fighters of a very good average size, sometimes running very large. The Clachan Beag hotel now controls the fishing there, as on all the other Barra lochs.

I used to borrow the doctor's little one-man boat on it, and with Donald at the oars I perched on the restricted space at the blunt end with my bottom regularly wetted if there were any wave at all. The doctor's boat is no longer there , but the bank fishing can be very good, especially in the evening.

However, my best fish, of over 2 lbs, came late one afternoon in April from the west bank near the island with its ruined castle. It took a size 10 Greenwell's Glory in a flurry of waves whipped up by that worst of winds, a north-easter. After it had been weighed with due ceremony on the Post Office scales I presented it to Mrs Maclean who, with her sister,used to run the hotel, as proof that I could occasionally catch fish. It was placed on an ashet (Scots for large plate — French "assiette") and borne in triumph by her through both bars. Drinks from her husband were on the house.

The telephone in the residents' bar rang. A call for me! "This is the Secretary of the Barra Angling Association. A person answering your description was seen poaching on Loch Tangusdale this afternoon and illegally removing a large trout!" For at least five seconds I was horribly convinced — what a headline it would make in the Stornoway Gazette — but it was only Reg Allan employing his dramatic talents to terrifying effect. After the "Ferry Likely" incident, I should have realised the efficiency of the heather telegraph and the perfect dramatic timing which lies at the heart of the Barra sense of humour.

Loch Tangusdale can be fished with the same flies as Loch an Duin, but 10s are often better in the spring, and the Ombudsman is an excellent tail fly from a boat. Do use 5 or 6 lb nylon for your evening leaders when the really big ones (much bigger than my best) wallop about. Greenwell's, March Brown and Blue Zulu should be added to the flies already mentioned.

I have written about Barra, seduced no doubt, by its own very special charm, but the other islands have much more extensive and often famous fishings of their own. Anyone visiting the Western Isles for a trout-fishing holiday will everywhere experience the wonderful freedom of having literally hundreds of lochs to choose from. Trout fishing is mainly free, or to be had for the polite asking or the payment of a modest fee. The angler's landscape is a constantly changing delight, and the bird population is huge and varied. The weather alternates between balmy breezes and strong winds (which often bring up the big ones). Splendid sea trout and salmon fishing is available by booking well ahead through advertisements in the angling press. Everyone is sympathetically helpful to anglers, rejoicing with them that rejoice and ready to weep with them that weep after a bad day, but always positively eager to put the visitor on to a good loch.

The charm of Hebridean fishing lies in all of these, but don't ask me to distil it into something simple. If you learn to expect the unexpected you will have the beginnings of its understanding and appreciation. The weather is changeable but, as the wise Irish gillie is alleged to have said about salmon fishing, "Any change in the weather is a change for the better even if it's for the worse." With that philosophy, you can't go far wrong here.

Mill Loch, South Uist (brown trout, salmon and seatrout)

Lower Kildonan (salmon and seatrout), South Uist

Loch Roag (salmon and seatrout), South Uist

Lower Kildonan, South Uist

Photos: Courtesy of Capt. John Kennedy, Lochboisdale

Chapter 2

INDIAN Army colonels of the old school have had a bad press, but this is almost wholly undeserved. But they did try to live up to their cartoon image from time to time, and obviously derived much pleasure from it. They appear in the diary, for even in wartime I managed to keep my diary going, though opportunities to fish were few and far between. Diarykeeping was strictly forbidden, in case the enemy got a hold of your private thoughts and thus found a way to win the war from them. How odd that, after the war, so many generals unblushingly published their memoirs based on their own, presumably illegal, diaries!

During that war, at the age of nineteen, I passed out from the OTS Bangalore in South India and with three others travelled to Ootacamund in the Nilgiri Hills for a week's leave before being sent off to sample the delights of a Jungle Warfare Training Centre. At Metapallyam Junction we tried in vain to order breakfast at the station restaurant, but it was crowded with military men of much higher rank than we, and the bearers (waiters) simply ignored us.

Suddenly we were joined by a late arrival, a diminutive full colonel of the Indian Army, to our eyes straight out of a cartoon. When he realised that we had been shamefully overlooked and neglected he threw back his head and bayed, "Bay-rerrrrr!" All over the restaurant there was the clatter of dropped plates and smashing glasses — the air shimmered round our table in the later style of the matter-transporter on the Starship "Enterprise", clearing to reveal twelve bearers standing quivering to attention with order pads and pencils poised.

We had a splendid breakfast. Replete, the Colonel surveyed us with a twinkle in his eye. "Been out long?" he bellowed. "Six months, sir", we quavered. "Thought so", he replied with satisfaction. "Look a bit pink, what!'

We all boarded the little train for Ooty, sharing a carriage with the Colonel and a friendly GSTP (Gin Swilling Tea Planter) who initiated us into the delights of this incomparable railway. "Fancy a spot of tea?" he suggested. "Leave it to me.

He summoned a railway company bearer who took our orders and phoned them up the line. At the next station more bearers swarmed aboard, giving each of us a beautifully laid out tray, including flowers, with cup, saucer and individual pot of excellent Nilgiri tea and a plate loaded with delectably sticky cakes. At the next station everything was efficiently whisked away after we had washed our hands in the bowls provided. Just what we were not used to.

The GSTP was helpful about fishing. "Go to the Nilgiri Game office in Ooty", said he. "They'll fix you up." Next day I did, and was kitted out with a Hardy's rod and Farlow's reel and line, supplied with two ponies and the services of a shikari (native guide) for the morrow, and all well within my meagre pay. With two casts of Clyde "wee flees" in my pocket, a gift from my brother when I was on embarkation leave, I was well equipped for a wonderful day on the Mekod, about six miles over rolling country. It resembled a large Scottish burn, or rather "water", of a type I was well used to at home. My casting was understandably rusty, but I soon had the trick of it: all I had to do was to wait for a cloud to go over the sun and the trout would rise, and the Clyde flies proved once more that they will take trout anywhere.

The only bad moment of a great day was when we were passing through a very jungly bit of country and the shikari observed brightly, "Very good tiger country, sahib!"

All the guests at our little hotel had trout for the fish course that evening. The Colonel expressed his amazed appreciation. "You've even managed to see that I got a double ration", said he gratefully between mouthfuls. "That's for getting us our breakfast", I replied.

I have associated Indian Army colonels with successful fishing ever since. How right I was!

Thank you, Colonel Sahib

Having been brought up in the hard school of upper Clyde and Tweed, I knew nothing about loch fishing when I first came to live in the Western Isles. My best friends tell me still that nothing has changed. However, I had to adjust from river to loch fishing, and it was difficult.

I was given lots of advice, mostly contradictory, and searched in vain for some simple, clear, authoritative (not authoritarian) written guidance. Most of the books available were helpful in parts, albeit somewhat dated, and I picked up some useful ideas from them along with some very suspect dogma. Some were gloriously ludicrous both in content and style, discursive to the point of self-indulgence and often pompous beyond belief. One reduced me to helpless giggles every time the author solemnly informed his readers: "We then partook of our sandwiches". In more ways than one, most of them belonged to a bygone age, and they did not inspire confidence in someone as ignorant as I. (Incidentally, I now collect such books, for the simple delight in fishing and sublime innocence of their authors are curiously attractive.)

Sidney Spencer's "The Art of Lake Fishing (with Sunk Fly)" (Witherby, 1934) and Colonel Joscelyn Lane's " Lake and Loch Fishing (Seeley Service — no date) were very useful, as was H P Henzell's "The Art and Craft of Loch Fishing" (Philip Allan, 1937). The works of R C Bridgett were wonderfully evocative accounts of loch fishing, but the instruction was incidental and the prose somewhat over-genteel. What I desperately sought, however, was a primer on how to go about it — a beginner's (in my case idiot's) guide, to be supplemented before tackling the best of the other books I have mentioned. I found the gem I was seeking in the reserve stock of our excellent local library, and have since bought my own copy: "Loch Trout", by Colonel H A Oatts (Herbert Jenkins, 1958). It is still fairly easily available from most angling book specialists, and at a modest price.

The title is typical of the whole book — short, brisk and always to the point. The author, Colonel Henry Augustus Oatts, was born in Roslin, Midlothian, in 1898, attended Bedford School and the Royal Military Academy, served in India, contributed to "The Field", and wrote his book from Cuil lodge, Kilmelfort, Argyll. That is all I have been able to find out about him. I wish I had met him, if only to thank him for writing the kind of book I then badly needed and still use with profit, and for providing a model for anyone attempting a book of instruction which is also both enjoyable and inspirational.

The book has all the virtues and none of the vices of a military man's writing. Oatts has clear ideas of the objective — to convey information easily and effectively in an engagingly pleasant way without waffle. The instruction is easy to follow, and it is illustrated by some lovely stories, totally relevant to the point being made, which remain in the mind at the lochside when the theory is being put into practice by the reader. Oatts would have made an excellent teacher.

As befits a military man, he is very good on tactics, on the "approach" to the loch, on how to read it, on the wisdom of standing well back for your first cast so that you cover trout lying close in. Here the author's own line drawings (which look like plans of attack!) are particularly clear and helpful. The beginner will find his systematic approach to bank fishing of real value.

The photographs, taken by a friend, catch exactly the flavour of the book. Unfortunately, some of them show the author standing up in a boat, after he has told us that "Standing up in a boat is silly", but he does explain that it is permissible after fishing from a sitting position if the boat is anchored and the background provides sufficient camouflage. I remain unconvinced.

Beginners can ignore much of his advice on tackle as being outdated since the post-war technological revolution in the tackle trade, but his basic principles are still very sound. He is very good on the benefits of a long, tapered leader (at a time when most anglers used untapered ones of no more than nine feet). Oatts rejects the idea that there is an optimum size or weight of rod. What is important is that it should "fit" the angler. My favourite quotation from this section , advice badly needed in an age of rampaging gadgeteering, is: "Fishing tackle cannot be too simple". The photographs show him clad in a dull, drab raincoat and hat, a wide-mouthed simple net slung over his shoulder — the whole image that of an old, grey heron, motionless at the lochside. "Quick, jerky movement is fatal in all forms of shikar" reminds us that in fishing for wild brown trout we are hunters, and have to behave as such.

The core of the book is "approach", and Oatts illustrates this by his description of catching, through the application of sound military principles, the biggest trout of his life, a cannibal that had to be removed, lurking in an almost inaccessible place in the loch. "There was nothing particularly clever or skilful about this, and I quote it as an example of choosing the right method. Regular Army officers are often good fishermen, and the reason may well be that they are (or were!) trained to appreciate any given situation or problem in terms of Object — Factors affecting the attainment of the object — Choice of method — Plan. Few fish can hold out against that sort of thing for long!" The gentle, mildly ironic diffidence of this is typical of the book, and it is equally typical that Oatts doesn't even mention the weight of this record trout.

Oatts is a trustworthy guide on flies. While conceding that some flies work for some fishers and not for others, and that there are mysterious variations in their effectiveness from one district to another, he provides a list which is both sound and thought-provoking, and the comments are often memorable: "The Mallard and Claret is a long-service, steady old soldier, like the Pivot Man of Waterloo days, and often wins or saves the day for a loch fisherman". And on the March Brown: "There is no better fly for loch trout — anywhere — anytime — any position on the cast. A well-worn March Brown is a real treasure". Unfortunately, Oatts doesn't give us the precise dressings — even among "traditional" flies there is some variation — though he does occasionally highlight a feature as in the Grouse and Green whose green "should be a good dark green", which agrees very well with the opinions of a modern writer, Stan Headley of Orkney, who recommends bottle green as an effective, yet apparently unlikely fly colour.

The few stories are tellingly brief, sometimes marvellously funny, and always to the point, leaving the reader wishing for more. To illustrate the mystery of the effects of sound rather than simple vibration on fish, he contrasts the immediate result of his nailed boot scraping on a stone on fish in a nearby pool in Waziristan which had paid no attention to a mountain battery firing eighty yards away, with his experience elsewhere, in an Indian Native State, where he saw fish regularly coming to be fed when temple bells sounded. The best is the tale of the retired Indian Army colonel who firmly believed in shouting at the top of his voice, assisted by his gillie, an ex-Guards sergeant-major, whenever he hooked a salmon, convinced that the row confused the fish and led it to over-tax its strength: "The salmon leapt and I leapt, cattle stampeded and birds migrated, and had we been anywhere near Wellington Barracks some of the windows must have been broken ...". And the stentorian pair had three salmon, one after the other, while Oatts had his hands clapped over his ears. I have always meant to try this, but none of my friends has volunteered to act as gillie.

There are good chapters on the trout itself; the weather — very sensible on sheep uphill (good) downhill (less), at the bottoms of sheltered glens (go home!); and one on "Relatives" (salmon and sea-trout) which is full of good sense. There is also a simple, clear (how often the word comes to mind while reading the book!) glossary which is of huge benefit to the absolute beginner. I often forget that "bob fly" is a technical term and fail to explain it to a beginner. Oatts doesn't.

The often wearisome cliches of proverbial advice get short shrift. Oatts describes his problems with an awkward little lochan where the wind was unusually contrary. He learned not to exhaust himself fighting the wind and flogging the water, but to watch for moving fish and the right time to cast. "The old teaching that the way to catch fish is to keep the flies on the water and your eyes on the flies is only half the truth, and is not a very intelligent approach to any form of fishing."

The book, as I have said, is much more than instructional. It is full of the author's love of wild places and the solitary delights of loch fishing, something which appeals more and more to anglers from the south, if the number of refugees who appear at my door every season is anything to go by. There is no sentimentality in this. Oatts simply remarks that, after many years of fishing abroad for all kinds of fish, often of the highest class, he came back to loch fishing with relief: "... once a fisherman gets the feel of it (loch fishing) nothing else seems quite as good .... just the wild beauty of the loch and the skill and wits of the fisherman. The loch mind is the mind of a man who prefers a basket of half-pounders among the hills to a twenty-pounder from behind the gas-works ..."

Of course, the economics of book production demand that angling books have to be slanted in the direction of the largest potential sales, hence the number of books on reservoir fishing, but perhaps the growing movement north and west of angling migrants each summer deserves a new book on loch fishing, incorporating the best relevant developments in stillwater angling in the south with the best of our own developing practice in the north.

Do not for one moment be put off the book by imagining that the author is some kind of old-fashioned Colonel Blimp figure from a David Lowe cartoon. I don't know whether Oatts was Indian Army or British Army in India, but a long time ago I also served, though briefly, under the Raj — and all the Indian Army colonels I met were invariably gentle and courteous men, quite unlike their cartoon representations, unless they were deliberately poking fun at themselves (which they frequently did). This is still, after 36 years, a genuinely valuable book, and not just for the beginner, written with clarity and gentle wit, and with a wonderfully sensitive appreciation of the satisfactions of loch fishing then and now.

Chapter 3

THE following may perhaps look like an idealised picture of the benefits of cooperation between two anglers sharing a loch boat so that each enjoys to the full the delights of this style of fishing. But it was not always so. My diary records the essentials of the long chats I used to have with professional gillies who taught me much about gillying and fishing, but it was their stories of the oddities of some of their guests that fascinated me even more. The notion of selflessly helping your boat partner to success was, alas, foreign to the nature of some.

A then beginner gillie, under tuition from one more experienced, was warned of the strange behaviour of two regular guests for whom the term "love-hate relationship" might have been invented, though with more hate than love. The pair always fished together, sitting side by side on the fishing plank at the stern of the boat and taking alternate 15-minute turns at fishing. Precisely at the end of the first 15-minute spell the unmistakable ringing of a kitchen timer rent the silence of the loch, bewildering the novice gillie — and the other man started fishing before the echoes had died away. This was their method of ensuring that each had exactly the same fishing time as the other so that none gained an advantage over the other. And each hated it when the other had a fish.

Another eccentric, obviously with all the advantages of a classical education, always carried a bottle of whisky with him and, as the boat was rowed out from the jetty, uncorked it and poured a libation into the water, muttering a prayer in Ancient Greek to the presiding deities of the loch beseeching success to his rod. (Which gods in the pantheon look after salmon fishers, I wonder?) Anyway, no libation was poured for the gillies. The classicist thereafter spent his day being gillied over water where no salmon had been seen in living memory. There was no divine intervention from Olympus.

We order things better nowadays.

Boat fishing, Hebridean style, may be new to the visitor. This absorbing branch of angling can be enjoyed by everyone, and it can certainly prolong active angling life for the veterans who may have some difficulty in bank fishing.

Two men in a boat

(It could, of course, be two women, or a man and a woman. The same principles apply.)

The excitement and fun we get out of fishing, as well as the less enjoyable emotions, can be experienced in every part of our sport on river, loch, reservoir or small fishery. I am personally addicted to wending my solitary way over the moor to fish remote loch or spate river in splendid solitude, and I used to be equally addicted to single-handed boat fishing for all our game fish, but I am beginning to believe that one of the most deeply satisfying kinds of fishing comes from the cooperation of two anglers in a boat, fishing for sea trout and salmon.

In more spacious days the angler would have an attendant, a boatman or gillie to row the boat and place him where the fish were to be found, someone who would take all the physical labour to himself while unobtrusively guiding and advising. Some of us would have been on the laird's plank at the blunt end; others — I know my place — would have been at the oars. It may be heresy to suggest it, but we order things much better today when many of us have discovered that the delights of boat fishing are enhanced by sharing the two roles. But remember, if you are new to loch fishing in unfamiliar waters, that if you can hire a gillie who knows the loch you are making a wise investment both in learning the skills of boat-handling and how to fish in the special conditions of that particular loch.

I was lucky enough to get to know the last of the traditional gillies of these parts, now disappeared through the social and economic changes of the past twenty years, when I first began to fish our club loch both singlehanded or with a friend, and talk with some of the gillies at the lunch break. Occasionally I was myself gillied by them and saw at first hand what skills were necessary to make the boat creep up to a salmon lie without splash of oar or rattle of rowlock, the gillie positioning it so that the angler could cast at the angle easiest for him and most suitable to his abilities. I doubt if some of the less experienced anglers ever appreciated the delicate skills displayed in all this, but the veterans certainly did. These gillies were crofters, supplementing a low income by summer gillying and going back to work the croft in the evening before another hard day at the oars. They were men of real virtue (in the old Roman sense) who took great but quiet pride in doing a job really well while being subservient to no-one. Their young successors are often very good, but may be comparative transients in the job, and thus haven't a lifetime's applied experience behind them.

Older and more experienced club members added to my education in the unobtrusive skills of boat handling and fish spotting, skills very different from the equally specialised techniques of handling a boat on a big reservoir, as I discovered when in turn passing on my experience to a former reservoir man now settled here. (I remember his delight at the discovery of the civilised and leisurely lunch-break on lochside or island which we share with our Irish cousins.) I still can't do some of the things the old gillies could, or at least nowhere near as well, but I keep trying and I keep learning.

Our system is simple. Each takes a half hour at the oars while the other fishes, Hebridean style, sitting on a plank across the stern area, and the boat is let down quietly and gently downwind so that the flies can cover the lies or the spot where a salmon has been seen to move. We also change immediately if a salmon is boated! Times are modified to suit conditions.

If a fish is hooked the bows of the boat are already pointing into the loch, and an awkward fish that takes off like a rocket can be at once followed without fuss. It is a deceptively simple method of fishing, but one capable of the most subtle modifications. It takes a lot of learning, especially the smooth and efficient cooperation in the changing roles of fisher and gillie, but that can also be a source of much innocent merriment.

The essence of it is that you must have a really good (I do mean morally good — at least in fishing terms) boat companion who genuinely wants you to catch fish. I am assuming that you are of the same high ethical standard and want him to do well too. If this is the case each can train the other in one's little idiosyncrasies — on how far away you like to fish the lie, on how able you are to cast over your left shoulder as well as your right, etc. What matters, and it is worth repeating, is that the gillie wants you, wills you, to succeed. So the triumphs are doubled and the disasters shared.

Loch salmon are like salmon everywhere — kittle cattle. They tend to lie near the lee shore (which the Hebridean style is designed to suit) and frequently must be enticed, more often irritated, into taking. Hugh Falkus is right about this in rivers, where persistence often pays, but it may be even more so in lochs. Salmon will often rise to your flies and turn away in disdain, or just not bother, but often they can be delicately badgered into aggressive suicide. The main thing is intelligent persistence, a varying of the angles of fly presentation, and a determination to come back later and try again when conditions are better or the sun has shifted to a more suitable angle. (Your splendid gillie has, of course, held the boat off the lie so that the fish has not been alarmed.)

As the fisher becomes older, this kind of fishing becomes more and more attractive. Even on rough days, often the best for salmon fishing, you can harbour your strength by taking it easy on the upwind bank over a cup of coffee while you keep an eye open for moving fish on the far shore, the cue for a quick descent on a possible taker before once more heading for more sheltered waters. You can carry all you need in the boat, protected from the wet by a clean fertiliser bag, and thus have total mobility. Our oldest club members, Fin and Dugald, did just that with great skill and cunning in the days of their partnership. They caught a lot of salmon and never seemed to break sweat. Alternating between fishing and gillying gives a rest from each activity, reducing fatigue while increasing interest and enjoyment. A day is a full day, in every sense of the word, and the sense of satisfaction in performing the dual roles of angler and gillie is a very profound one.

I have also finally decided, despite my lifelong love of wild brown trout fishing, that the take of a loch salmon on a single-handed rod is the most exciting thing in angling, and the excitement and delight are doubled by being shared with a friend. Contrariwise, when the line inexplicably goes slack, commiseration is immediate, and you have an appreciative audience for the light laugh or the stoical quip, however unconvincing the performance.

When a fish takes, the team swings into smooth action. You have complete trust in your man at the oars. He knows what to do, and does it. You can concentrate on the screaming reel and your own private terrors about the security of the hookhold. As the immediate excitement dies down the gillie invariably remarks in a casually conversational tone that his job in loch fishing is far more important than that of the angler, and that you wouldn't have hooked the fish but for his finely honed skills. It is a familiar litany, one capable of infinite elaboration, and the satisfaction of a successful netting brings even more paeans of self-praise from the man at the oars. Hilarity reigns, and you store up your retaliation for when he in turn boats his salmon.

The fish is dispatched and slid into the wetted salmon bass, the boat rapidly tidied, the gillie's rod stored safely, and fisher and gillie change places — and personalities. You keep low as you change. Standing up in a boat in open water is a short way to a watery grave, especially if you wear no buoyancy aid. (Why is the angling press full of photographs of idiots standing up in boats? The fish see them from further off, the angler has to cast longer and longer, and one moment of imbalance ......) But you both know the drill, and it is carried out swiftly and smoothly. Now you are the gillie, recently the successful fisher, and you concentrate on ensuring your companion's success, reminding him how fortunate he is to have such a paragon directing his operations.

The boat drill you have just carried out has been the product of discussion and experience. Little energy is dissipated on unessentials, for the taking time of the salmon is not to be wasted. Photographs can wait, and ceremonies of congratulation are best kept to the end of the day.

I used to know, and have fished with, the wrong sort of boat partners. They may have been outstanding human beings, but they were one and all menaces in a boat. Experience is said to teach fools (since they require it in order to discover the obvious), but real fools never learn and just go on driving the rest of us insane. Better to avoid them if you wish to retain your sanity and your life. But when you have found sound and sensible boat companions then grapple them to your soul with hoops of steel.

Two men in a boat can bring you some of the greatest and most satisfying moments in fishing. With a well-found and well-ordered boat with all clutter tidied away, rowlocks tied in and everything in its place, boat fishing is a continuing delight even if you catch nothing.

And there is a final benefit. The role-changing is good for you and can make you a better fisher. A change is as good as a rest. You develop new skills, spot fish you would never see if it were your turn to fish, and generally become more relaxedly alert to your surroundings. You are just as much a hunter as the man fishing, perhaps even more so. To spot a low head-and-tailer at fifty yards, to put the boat quickly and quietly upwind of it, to see your companion (who, concentrating on his own fishing never saw the fish) place his flies over the spot, having followed your precise directions (I'm glad I learned long ago the Army's system of "Right, two o'clock ", and I teach it to my friends), and finally to see the line draw away as the fish takes — all this and fishing too — is to enjoy your day to the fullest.

Our forebears didn't know what they were missing by simply being chauffeured round a loch. Some things in fishing are better now than in the good old days, and we should make the most of them.

Chapter 4

A DISTINGUISHED Lewisman, James Shaw Grant, sometime owner and editor of the Stornoway Gazette and a perceptive writer on both the Western Isles and the world at large, once described the Lewisman as "a law-abiding anarchist". (This apercu went straight into the diary, for I at once saw its application to angling.) You have to be a Lewisman or to live in Lewis for a long time to appreciate the full implications of this superbly accurate definition, but it could easily be applied to anglers in general — at least the sensible ones — for the good angler at first obeys the rules his predecessors have laid down, but from time to time takes a good hard look at them and cheerfully breaks them if they don't continue to make sense. Deep down we all enjoy the exposure of the errors of some of the selfappointed high priests of angling, the realisation that the old gods have feet of clay, the demythologising of systems of belief which seem designed to prevent the operations of critical intelligence and simple common sense. There is a strong streak of the nonconformist in all good fishers. Indeed, if this book has a recurring theme, it is that we all, fishers and non-fishers alike, should cherish the best of the past while embracing the best of the new, in both fishing and life, subjecting both to continual critical analysis so that we can be confidently adult in our conclusions. We can leave it to our children to expose the deficiencies in our thinking.

Of course, totalitarian notions of angling are not the fault of the great figures of the past. Frederick Halford was not as purist as his disciples, who erected a rigid doctrine of dry fly angling on what they believed Halford stood for, and defended their cult with an almost religious zeal. The followers of "exact imitation" had their points, but it is a regrettable tendency of humanity to generalise, absolutise and finally fossilise attitudes into laws and regulations admitting of no exception. This makes insecure minds feel secure. Worse, it tends to encourage them to tyrannise over the rest of us .

Every so often the angling bigots give themselves away, to the huge amusement of the nonconformist majority. A splendid example is provided by the Muddler Minnow, imported from North America in the 1960's as a trout "fly" but over the past few years establishing itself as a great attractor and taker of loch salmon. Sir Gregor MacGregor of MacGregor tells of a fishing companion on the Grimersta who reacted to Sir Gregor's five salmon on a Black Muddler by exclaiming, "That's not a salmon fly. I wouldn't use one of those!" Nothing illustrates better the bone-headedness of those anglers who believe that somewhere in the past everything was laid down for posterity to follow uncritically. One wonders if such are really anglers or whether they pursue our sport because they believe it confers on them some kind of social status, rather than being the obsessively driven individuals that the rest of us are.

The Ombudsman, despite its doubtful parentage or perhaps because of it, comes therefore as a boon and a blessing to all of us who are in angling terms "law-abiding anarchists" and who modestly regard ourselves as among the regenerate and rightminded of humanity!

The Hebridean Ombudsman

A long time ago I was persuaded into passing on my limited skills in fly-dressing to adult beginners at a very loosely organised "club" which, since then, has met once a week during winter evenings.

It began with a few keen friends who found to their delight that fly-dressing was much easier than they had been led to believe. They are now old lags, who come back each winter to tie flies, swap materials, pass on ideas and generally keep in touch during the fishless season. Each year new beginners appear and are caught up in the excitement of learning a new skill, eventually to enjoy the keenest of angling pleasures, that of catching fish on flies of their own tying.

I make a point of introducing unusual, but successful, dressings to the beginners once they have mastered the basics and, apart from the shocked hilarity occasioned by their first tying of the Muddler Minnow — how does the deerhair spin like that? — their biggest moment of appalled disbelief comes when, having heard the principles of delicacy and restraint stressed again and again, they encounter the heretical, rule-breaking anarchy of Brian Clarke's Ombudsman.

Readers of "The Pursuit of Stillwater Trout" will remember that the author introduces the Ombudsman as a kind of generalised creepy-crawly, something to be trickled over the bottom of lake or reservoir as a general representation of lake-floor life, red in mandible and claw.

Here in our boulder-strewn island lochs, this tactic leads inevitably to becoming hung up on lumps of immovable Lewisian gneiss; but the Ombudsman has developed its own band of dedicated Hebridean devotees since some of us discovered other applications more suitable to wilder waters.

Tied on a long-shanked size 10 hook it is a superb fly for fishing on a short leader across or into the wind on a lee shore on which the waves are breaking and stirring up the bottom life, especially in early season but also all through the summer. Takes are definite, the rod tip dips firmly, and the brown trout are usually bigger than average and in better condition. There seems to be no hesitation in the take — no delicate knockings, just full-blooded thumps.

Again on an LS 10 hook it is an excellent point fly when fishing a team of flies from a drifting boat. Here in the islands we have to prospect for our fish, and the Ombudsman searches the water well, having the extra weight of the LS hook to take the flies down to the fish and to stabilise the whole leader in the manner of the "stretcher" of our loch-fishing ancestors, thus helping the other flies to fish properly. Again it seems to take the biggest trout. If required, it can be weighted under the dressing, but in our often shallow lochs this must be done with restraint.

A single weighted Ombudsman, however, can produce surprises if cast into one of the many mysterious little patches of water which dot our moors and have no reputation for producing fish. A visiting friend, passing by one such on his way to a "proper" loch one day, did just this, and landed a beautiful three-pounder.

John M (so called to distinguish him from the myriad Macleods of Lewis) has almost always one on the tail of a three-fly leader. On one difficult evening in low wind we each had three trout, picked up as we drifted down the lee of some little islands, but those he took on the Ombudsman dwarfed mine, taken on a more conventional and much smaller tail fly. I would never have dreamed of using such a big fly in the conditions, but I have learned my lesson. Ken, now in the Orkneys, used to fish it on an LS 8 hook as a bob (!) fly, and he caught many fish on it by rapping it down on the surface as if to call attention to itself. I wonder if he still does? It is not a tactic for lesser mortals, but it often worked spectacularly for him.

Another Ken, a keen and skilful golfer, became an equally fine fly-fisher who now regularly takes salmon from the River Creed, which flows into the harbour at Stornoway. One day, having run through the contents of his fly boxes without result, he did what none of us with greater experience would ever have considered: he put on an LS 10 Ombudsman which he had learned to tie the previous winter and, inevitably, caught the only salmon taken from the river that day.

You will find the dressing in the chapter on flies. As this is the supreme illegitimate among trout flies you can vary the dressing as much as you wish without offending aesthetics or respectability. Make the head bulbous with mid to light-brown sewing thread. Do not restrain yourself. Ugliness is what you are after. Beauty is in the eye of the beholder, the only one that counts — in this case, the trout.

If you feel, having tied it, that it is all too much, and that you probably need to lie down quietly in a darkened room to recover, remember that it probably represents a dragonfly nymph. When you have seen the size of our Hebridean dragonflies you will appreciate that the nymphs are correspondingly enormous (they eat small fish!) and the Ombudsman can then be rationalised into something approaching exact imitation, though this is a casuistry probably not to be advanced in the presence of the neo-Halfordians of the chalk steams. Decidedly not recommended for the Test.

This is no one-season wonder. We have been using it here ever since it was nightmared up. But please use some restraint, despite what has just been written. In your modifications do not add a split shot under its awful head and give it a marabou tail, thus producing an Ombudsnobbler. If you do, may you wake up in the dead vast and middle of the night, screaming. One must draw the line somewhere.

Mind you, it just might work . . .

Chapter 5

IN Courtney Williams' "A Dictionary of Trout Flies" there is a short but very important chapter, 'On Maintaining the Purity of the Breed", which is a plea for an agreed standard when naming a fly. Thus, a Peter Ross is one dressed in the accepted and traditional manner; any variation in this dressing should properly be referred to as "Peter Ross (Variation)" so that we know where we are. Williams fully realised that such a variation dressing might be an even better fly than the original on certain occasions, but if we don't know what dressing a writer is referring to when he mentions the Peter Ross we are left in confusion.

This, of course, is by no means an argument against developing a standard fly further. Our "traditional" flies have arrived at that status after years, even centuries, of modification; but once the name is given we should stick to that name for that precise fly. If the changes are great enough we can give a new name to what is now a new fly.

With this caveat, we as anglers can happily accept our very human trait of being unable to leave well alone, and one which can lead us either to disaster or to new and beneficial insights in the development of fly patterns.

The two flies dealt with here exemplify our own good sense as anglers. We have left the Donegal Blue alone, apart from permissible variations in the depth of colour of the body, themselves arrived at in various places over a period of time. Harold's Grouse and Claret is an inspired and deliberate variation of the old Grouse and Claret. As its name suggests, the new fly does not replace the older; it intelligently modifies an already great fly to give us what I and others consider another great fly, and there is no confusion of name between them. I happily use each of them on different occasions. Nothing wrong with that, and it leaves us in a satisfyingly smug state of mind — something rare among anglers!

Claret and Blue

As well as the Ombudsman, I introduce my fly-dressing club to two other less well-known flies at an early stage in their progress partly because they are easy to tie, thus increasing the beginners' confidence, and because they are really and truly deadly for sea trout and salmon in our lochs. I can honestly say that both are mounted on my first leader of the day on any sea trout loch.

Again these patterns, at least for me, have their origins in angling literature though in books more difficult to obtain than 'The Pursuit of Stillwater Trout" which gave us the Ombudsman.

The Donegal Blue first came to my notice in the late Sidney Spencer's "Ways of Fishing" (Witherby, 1972) where he says: "I have no record of the true dressing of the Donegal Blue and I have never seen or heard of one differing from those I have fished for some years. It's a fly with, in suitable conditions, a kind of magic about it. Salmon, sea trout and brown trout take it avidly in a reasonable range of water colours and heights, and I have seen salmon slash savagely at it even on a blue day". He goes on to recommend it as a bob fly rather than a middle dropper or tail, then gives the dressing as he knows it:

Body: Coarse wool of a rather faded medium blue. Rib: A few turns of broad silver tinsel. Hackle: Black hen fibres, soft and of medium length

It has neither wing nor tail, though there is a Robert Mc Haffie dressing with a GP topping tail and a bronze mallard wing for summer salmon in rivers.

However, E J Malone's splendid and authoritative book, "Irish Trout and Salmon Flies (Colin Smythe, Ltd, 1984), gives the original dressing as one with a dark blue seal's fur body; and royal blue is recommended by at least one modern authority. Nevertheless, I have used Sidney Spencer's dressing, but with a teal blue seal's fur body and Veniard's flat silver tinsel No 3 as a rib for trout hooks 12, 10 and 8, and No 4 for larger sizes, for many years and with total satisfaction. A royal blue body seems to work just as well, and my friends now report great success with the original dark blue version. Perhaps you should try them all. Do give the body a good scrub with velcro, an old toothbrush or one of the sophisticated modern tools designed for the purpose. Spencer frequently remarks that most people fish too large on Hebridean lochs. He usually fished size 9 or

10 salmon irons except in a big wave, and the Donegal Blue fits into this range. My favourite hook is trout size 8, going up to 6 in a big blow and down as far as 12 in calmer waters. The tradition is different on the Grimersta (big bob fly, small tail fly) but it's the small tail fly that takes most of the salmon.

Nor should we always accept Spencer's insistence that it is purely a bob fly. My elder daughter, back home after some fishingless years overseas and slightly out of touch with fly names, completely outfished me twice running (not an unusual experience), taking all her fish on the tail fly. It was, of course, the Donegal Blue, which she had put on in mistake for another excellent blue fly, the Camasunary Killer.

It works well for brown trout on the "blue body, black hackle" principle of some old Irish and Scottish flies, referred to by Kingsmill Moore in "A Man May Fish". You will also find its double in the Blue Label, a Loch Lomond sea trout and salmon fly, recommended by the late Bill McEwan.

No one fishing the salmon and sea trout lochs of the Hebrides and Ireland should fail to read and read again Sidney Spencer's books. Like his description of the Donegal Blue there is a magic about them. Who could resist titles like "Salmon and Sea Trout in Wild Places" and "Newly from the Sea"? They are a perfect complement to Kingsmill Moore's classic.

Harold's Grouse and Claret appeared in a most interesting book by Douglas C Townsend, "Fly Tying with Harold Howorth" (Adam and Charles Black, 1980). The book is now out of print but it deserves a new edition. It contains a most attractive portrait of Harold Howorth, a north of England fly-dresser of rare quality, and it gives the dressings of his flies, several of which I have happily confirmed to be highly effective in our waters.   Some are very intelligent modifications of traditional patterns, such as his Grouse and Claret, in the same class as the Donegal Blue, and there can be no higher praise than that.

The fly was developed for sea trout fishing after, as the author describes, Mr Howorth's standard Grouse and Claret had lost its wing to a large fish but went on to attract more sea trout than before. There followed a long period of experimenting before the variation pattern was finally settled.

The fly is perfect as a mid-dropper or, even better, as a point fly. In the water the grouse hackle gives it the straggly appearance of life, enhanced by the long-recognised glow of the traditional Grouse and Claret — a combination of the gold rib and the claret seal's fur. Following Kingsmill Moore, I prefer to rib the body in the same direction as the body dubbing so that the rib becomes buried in the body material and adds to the translucent effect, increased by roughing up the body as with the Donegal Blue.   It is an excellent brown trout fly as well, and dressed on a size 10 trout hook it once produced for me a totally unexpected (and undeserved) salmon from a scarcely rippled loch. Best of all, it has been especially

successful in taking what is often the only sea trout on difficult or near-impossible days, both in clear and peaty water. Harold Howorth's dressing has the simplicity of most truly great flies:
  Hook: 10 - 8 Silk: Black
  Tail: Small piece of yellow wool, fluffed out
  Rib: Oval gold
  Body: Dark claret wool (I prefer seal's fur), well roughened
  Thorax: Single strand bronze peacock herl, two or three turns
  Hackle: Grouse neck feather wound as bushy as possible.

Douglas Townsend says that he used the fly for ten years prior to writing his book. Clearly it has stood the test of time and deserves to be better known.

The Donegal Blue and Harold's Grouse and Claret working in unison once helped to give me the happiest fishing day of my life. (See Chapter 10 "Once in a Lifetime"). May they help you too.

Chapter 6

I HAVE always kept a gardening diary for much the same reasons as I have always kept a fishing diary. Sometimes the experiences recorded in each chime together, one illuminating the other.

Long go, when we lived on the mainland and had just moved into our first house, we had an insufferable neighbour who knew everything. Our garden had never been properly cultivated, probably because its intractable boulder clay was very near the surface. As I attacked the gluey mess with a spade, I reflected on the "Punch" parody of "Popular Gardening" with its bright little piece by a consultant psychiatrist solemnly entitled, "The Correlation between Boulder Clay Soil and the Suicide Rate".

At this low moment in my gardening life my awful neighbour leaned over the fence and declared with all the pompous authority of the seriously ignorant, "You'll never grow vegetables in that soil. I've tried it. It's impossible." Having put me in my place, he departed, smirking. I glowered at the retreating figure and muttered several things under my breath including, "We'll see".

I sought advice from a doctor neighbour who had long experience of my boorish gardening expert. "That one", he declared with clinical relish, " suffers from mental constipation and verbal diahorrea. You will simply have to prove him wrong. Go to it."

So I did, pouring manure, compost, weathered boiler ash, mature sewage sludge and other unmentionables into the soil. It took two years, but the garden responded magnificently, and that summer the turnips,

FISHER IN THE WEST

Scaladale River.

Brown Trout 4lbs, caught on size 12 Black Spider. Photo: Norman Mackenzie

Brown Trout, South Lochs.
Photo: Dr. Boyd Peters

FISHER IN THE WEST

Peter Ross

Arctic Charr (Salvelinus Alpinus)

Loch Carason, Uig

peas, cabbages and carrots were a joy to behold. Oddly enough, my neighbour thereafter disappeared rapidly into the house the moment I appeared in the garden.

So with angling absolutists, for there are some — very few, but they make up for their lack of numbers by turning up the volume. The Peter Ross is still something of a mystery fly, and my fishing diary records how many otherwise sensible anglers have told me how they have failed with it. The true absolutists (never native Hebridean), the ones suffering from the same complaints as my erstwhile neighbour, have of course gone further and told me that I will "never" catch anything with it.

But this is one of the greatest of loch flies for all our game fish in the Hebrides and my own first choice for salmon and sea trout in small rivers; so my advice to all of those who claim they can't catch fish with it is the same as my old doctor's: "Go to it."

The Puzzle of the Peter Ross

Dugald was one of the great fishers of these parts, and his passing left us all grieving. Typically, it came within hours of gillying his great friend Fin on to the last salmon of the season. As a young bank apprentice in Killin, Dugald knew Peter Ross, a local shopkeeper who died in 1923 after suggesting the changes to the Teal and Red which gave us one of the most famous flies in the history of angling. Yet Dugald, who in a long retirement fished almost every day of the season for trout, sea trout and salmon, caught almost nothing on that pattern. Surely, we all believed, something of the magic should have rubbed off on someone who once knew the man behind the fly!

Dugald shared this unhappy distinction with many, including the great Richard Walker, who confessed in one of his articles in the angling press that he had never caught a trout on the Peter Ross, despite regularly giving it an extended trial each season. Yet surveys have shown that the fly does well on lowland reservoirs, and it's still a popular fly on lochs. Charles McLaren, in "The Art of Sea Trout Fishing" , had great confidence in it as a killer of both sea trout and salmon in loch and river — in fact it was a favourite of his.

The puzzle is that so many of my friends claim that it doesn't work for them. Is this just some kind of fashion? Is it the OK thing not to catch fish on the Peter Ross? But my friends are sensible people who do not go in for the striking of attitudes, especially in such a serious matter as fishing, and Richard Walker has left us all in his debt in his writings, the product of a clear-headed intelligence, entirely devoid of such flannel.

When I first came to live in the Western Isles I caught my first Lewis trout on a Peter Ross. Then followed years of frustration and total failure to catch anything on it. Like Richard Walker, I avoided the obvious trap of not including it on my leader then claiming it didn't work! Each season it had more than its fair share of chances to impress. Result: nil.

Then I tried it out on estuary sea trout and found it easily my best fly! On a size 12 hook, fished on the bob or tail of a two-fly cast, it was as near to a totally reliable fly as I could imagine. Incidentally, on the advice of John M , I now fish the Peter Ross on the tail with a simple Brown and Peacock Spider on the bob for estuary sea trout. It is a combination to be recommended.

As for the brown trout, everything changed some years ago when a shooting friend presented me with some beautifully marked teal flank feathers, unlike some of the stuff one sometimes receives from the wrong type of supplier. I tied up some size 12s for estuary fishing but decided first to try the fly once more for brown trout. Result: a huge success. On its first trial, one of my friends found me sitting in a state of shock on a lochside boulder. "There, there," he murmured, "losing a trout is not the end of the world." I shook my head dumbly and pointed to the magnificently beautiful trout on the rock beside me. (It was under a pound, but to me it was more than a thing of beauty, but rather one of life's great turning points.) I blurted out, "I haven't lost anything. I've just caught a trout on a Peter Ross!"

From then on it kept on working through the season and through every season since. Although previously most of my brown trout had been taken on the bob fly, usually on palmers — Zulus, Kate McLaren and the like — the wee Peter Ross on the tail was outfishing them all. Why? Was it the high-quality winging material, or was it simply the confidence I had gained from fishing with a really good-looking fly, even if it was one tied by myself? But on the day I caught that first of many trout on it I had no confidence (hence the ensuing state of collapse); and now, though I am forced back to using the pale imitations of decent teal feathers as before, the Peter Ross has maintained its dazzling form for six glorious years.

Moreover, during that seminal season and for the first time (though others had previously taken plenty), I caught salmon on the Peter Ross. Fishing my friend Aubrey's little spate river in August without result, I finally put on a Peter Ross dressed on a size 8 trout hook and, with no fish moving, tried it in a shallow pool where I had never previously seen a fish but where there was a nice streamy run under a peat bank. Normally one fishes this little pool from the "correct" side, casting over to the stream — but it had never worked for me. I was too idle to bother crossing to the other bank; so I stood well back, as one always must on such small, clear-water streams, and fished the "wrong" side. The fly was immediately taken in the middle of the pool by a fresh 7lb fish which gave me a hairy twelve minutes before I netted it out of fast water. I had to wade to the brim of my thigh waders to get at it, and it was my first truly eyeball-to-eyeball confrontation with a furious salmon. It was Hugh Falkus, in his excellent "Salmon Fishing", who advised the fishing of salmon pools from the "wrong" side. As usual, he was right. I now do it all the time.

My first salmon on the Peter Ross. Miracles indeed! But the best was yet to come. Early in October, after a rainless week, Aubrey phoned at breakfast with news of a flash flood during the night. By 10.30 am I was on the river, but with a fast-sinking heart, just like the water. Our spate rivers rise and fall rapidly, for their water comes straight off the hill, and this one runs over clean gravel on a steep course to the sea. You have to be quick — or so I believed at the time — and I was slow. The river was at low summer level and that, believe me, is low. Since I had driven a long way, I decided to fish anyway. I put up a trout cast with a single Peter Ross on a trout size 10 hook and pinned my hopes on the occasional sea trout, though there seemed to be nothing moving that morning.

Remembering my earlier success, I tried the same pool, now no more than two feet deep. No luck. So I went to the best pool on the river, which by this time had shrunk to the size of our kitchen (it's a small kitchen) and decided to try the earlier tactic of fishing it from the "wrong" side, from a high peat bank and a crouched position, peering cautiously over the edge like Mr Chad and hand-lining the fly in the sluggish current. Three times I raised what appeared to be a parr, and a small one at that. It took time for my slow brain to register that a parr would have had the fly first time. At the fourth cast the Peter Ross was taken with great delicacy by what proved to be a highly indignant 5 lb grilse, annoyed that anyone should have crept up on it in such an unsporting fashion.

It was impossible to land the fish from the high bank; so I slid down the peat bank at the tail of the pool to play the fish out from a safe wading position. Inevitably, in the slow motion beloved of producers of spaghetti westerns for their scenes of excessive and gratuitous violence, the peat bank collapsed. I fell flat on my back in two feet of water, throwing my rod aside to prevent a smash, and got thoroughly soaked from the neck downwards. I scrabbled frantically for the rod, found it, and lurched to my feet. Miraculously, the fish was still on.

Five minutes later — with water still brimming over the tops of my thigh waders, soaked to the skin and laughing insanely at the absurd triumph and ignominy of my situation — I slipped my net under the unluckiest salmon in Harris. Despite all the abuse it had suffered the little Peter Ross had held firm, thanks no doubt to its being dressed on a first-class hook, the Partridge Code A, in which for some seasons I have had complete trust.

The only witness to this was Uisgean's cow, a charming but rather forward lady who has the habit of silently approaching me from the rear, my hearing dulled by the sound of rushing waters, and breathing warmly down my neck when I believe myself to be alone in that wild and beautiful glen. Some day she'll have me in, but that day she didn't have to try, simply tossing her head in horror at the apparition squelching down the valley to hot coffee, a change of clothes, and hilarious sympathy and congratulations at Vanna and Aubrey's hospitable home.

Photographs were taken for the record before I drove off, clad in Aubrey's second-best gardening clothes, reflecting on what had turned out to be the year of the Peter Ross.

But the mystery, the puzzle, still remains, even after all those seasons of success with the fly. Is it the old story of an angler's style suiting one particular fly and not another? Is it that we give up using a fly after repeated failures and never use it again, claiming illogically that it doesn't catch fish for us? I doubt it. Richard Walker was too objectively scientific, and Dugald too sensible, for that.

The puzzle of the Peter Ross still nags at me despite, or perhaps because of, the happy seasons which have followed. I can only advance the theory that those excellent teal feathers gave me the confidence to use the fly in good conditions, rather than my putting it on in bad conditions then rapidly taking it off again. In other words, though convinced I was giving it a fair trial, I wasn't! As a fisher, my capacity for self-deception is boundless. Or should we abandon theorising and simply be left with our illusions and with those strangely comforting mysteries which surround the all-absorbing passion we call fishing?

Chapter 6

I HAVE remarked elsewhere on the angler's delight in proving the law-givers wrong and turning accepted wisdom on its head. Nowhere in angling is there more contradictory and confusing advice to beginner and experienced angler alike than in salmon fishing. There are very good books and very bad books on the subject, but almost all concentrate on fishing proper rivers with famous names, not the little spate streams with only a local reputation or none at all. This is unsurprising, considering the economics of the book market, for famous authors tend to be invited to famous rivers.

My own salmon angling was at first in rivers, but only in my youth when my trout fly was attacked by a salmon. I should have learned from that not so uncommon experience that summer salmon often take very small flies. Thereafter my salmon fishing was almost entirely loch fishing (where the fish again often take very small flies). But it was by a slow process of trial and (mainly) error that I managed to shed the weight of what might be claimed to be the accepted wisdom of salmon fishing and discovered that it didn't apply to very small streams.

It seems incredible now, after rereading the fishing diaries of many years, that I was so slow-witted in realising that different circumstances demand different tactics. The answer stared me in the face for years before I managed to throw off the accumulated wisdom of the ages and started to use my eyes — and brains — and remembered the long-forgotten lessons of my youth enshrined in early diary entries. Anyone who, like me, served his angling apprenticeship as a small boy fishing with worm and fly on moorland burns will have no problems with the tactics described here, though some bending and stretching exercises are recommended in advance for the more mature among us.

Salmon in Lilliput
A minor tactic for minor streams

I am not fortunate enough to fish the mighty salmon rivers of Scotland — Tweed, Tay, Dee and Spey — but probably have much more fun fishing our loch systems from boat or bank and our very few and often very small rivers. When I say "small" I mean it. Holiday anglers in Scotland are frequently advised to try our many spate rivers, but what is often passed by is the stream which is not much more than a burn. (In Scotland we classify running waters, in ascending order of size, as burns, "waters" and rivers.) What I refer to is unclassifiable — the smallest running water holding salmon — and it can contain unsuspected delights. The techniques for fishing it tend to break most of the established "rules", but they offer much pleasure to those who sensibly believe that rules are for the guidance of wise men and the obedience of fools. You can be a maverick while fishing with perfect propriety. You can have it both ways: you can regain your lost youth while apparently behaving like an old fool — but perhaps a successful old fool.

Let me describe my favourite little stream, typical of so many in the north, though uniquely attractive in my eyes.   It emerges from a small loch in a corrie high in the hills and runs for about four miles to the sea. It is fishable only for its last mile below a waterfall, the only obstacle faced by running fish. There are two "pools", one about the size of my garage and the other much smaller, and below them some nice little runs which at the right height of water can hold the odd fish. At the road bridge there is a maelstrom pool, almost unfishable with fly. A few fish are taken with the worm there and at the falls, but good fly water is scarce because the holding water is small, often thin, and always narrow. Even a moderate cast with a trout rod can easily have you hooked up in the heather on the opposite bank. The river runs beautifully clear as it drops, for though the glen is often ferociously boggy the river's course is over clean ice-age gravel, and it is fed in part by water running straight off the rocky hillsides, thus rising

Salmon Flies

Blue Elver

Stoats Tail

Silver Stoat
(Blue Hackle)

Sweep

Watson's Fancy

Hairy Mary

Gary Dog

Black Brahan

Kenny's Killer

Munro

Flashing Charmer

Thunder

Thunder (Var)

Muddler Minnow

Traditionals

Newcomers, Irish and Welsh

Clan Chief

Leven Spider

Maclean's Red Zulu

Charlie Maclean

Black Hopper

Mini-Muddler

Solicitor

Wee Peter

Bibio

Connemara Black

Claret Bumble

Golden Olive Dabbler

Golden Olive Bumble

Goat's Toe

Coch A Bonddu

Haul A Gwynt

Sooty Olive

Four favourites

Ombudsman
(see chapter 4)

Peter Ross
(see chapter 6)

Harolds Grouse
and Claret
(see chapter 5)

Donegal Blue
(see chapter 5)

and falling with the yo-yo rapidity of its kind. It is a very beautiful little stream and I have become very fond of it, though at first glance most fishers would never consider it as a salmon water, more a moorland trout stream, yet it has produced fish of over 10 lbs in the past and close to that in the present.

The problem is when to fish it. A full flood is impossible, yet in a few hours the water may appear to be equally impossibly low. Conventional fly fishing, therefore, presents all sorts of difficulties, added to which is the total absence of cover for the angler, requiring one to keep low and well back.

Through the kindness of the proprietor, my good friend Aubrey, I have fished this river for some years, though only intermittently and with equally intermittent success. I used conventional flies, and fished where possible in a falling water — which again restricted fishing time. Low water was considered near impossible for the reasons given above and for the added reason that low water can warm up quickly when the sun shines through our clear and unpolluted air, making fish torpid and disinclined to take. I used to believe, mistakenly, that it was essential to time things for somewhere between high flood and mid- drop, an impossibly fine timing unless you lived on the banks. Nowadays, I wait for a flood to bring up fish, and when I think there may be fish in the pools or runs I try my luck at any time thereafter, uninhibited by the previous restriction of being there at exactly the right time.

I found out how to fish the river almost by accident some years ago when I arrived at what should have been the perfect time after the forecasted heavy rain of the night before, except that the rain had missed the watershed and the river was impossibly low. Muttering maledictions at meteorologists and all their works I put up a Peter Ross, size 10 trout, on fine nylon and went in search of seatrout. In the best pool I raised a salmon three times (in my ignorance I thought the little flip in the water was caused by a parr) before it took the gently skittering just sub-surface fly. The fact that I then fell in (put not your trust on overhanging peat banks) but miraculously landed the fish (see Chapter 5 "The Puzzle of the Peter Ross") may have confused the message, though I did learn from the experience the usefulness of trout flies for summer salmon and had some success with them thereafter.

It was only after a few more seasons that the penny finally dropped in my inefficient brain (readers will be miles ahead by this time), when I realised that the river should be fished in the way I used to fish the burns of my youth for moorland trout. I settled on a size 10, single or double trout fly (Partridge Code A) or the remarkable Wilson Low Water doubles, size 16, on tackle fine enough not to discourage the fish but able to swim the fly without restriction and yet hold a wild, and often very surprised, salmon in a small pool. My leader had a butt of three feet of 15lb nylon, two feet of 11 lb and seven feet of Platil Universal Soft nylon which has a breaking strain of 9 lbs and the diameter of conventional 6lb nylon, yet it is not double strength nylon with all the dangers that might suggest. It may be considered too soft for normal fly fishing but it has worked perfectly for me for two seasons both in river and loch, where the 11lb can also be used. I could go lighter, but I am not keen on risking leaving fly and nylon in a fish just to boost my ego, though I will certainly reduce the fly size even further if I ever find it necessary.

I use a ten-foot trout rod, AFTM 6-8, with a neutral density FT7 line (a floater would probably be just as good, but I nowadays tend to use a very slow-sinking neutral density line for nearly everything), the comparatively heavy line necessary for the casting conditions. The built- in extension butt of this rod is a great comfort when playing a fish, as is the case with its big brother, the 11 foot version, which is my favourite loch rod for salmon. An ordinary 10 foot trout rod, AFTM 6-7, proved just as good, but it lacked the useful extension handle.

I simply keep well down, hugging the bank and staying as far back as I can, then cast **straight down** the pool and work the fly back **against** the current, such as it is, in little jerks or skitters very close to the surface. Sometimes this involves deep wading (almost up to my knees!) and hiding behind a boulder in midstream. You learn from experience where the fish like to lie, and in a small pool they can be in unexpected places. The fish take exactly like trout — a little flip on the surface and you strike **at once,** just as you would for small wild brown trout. A late tightening might work just as well, however. Concentrating on the taking strip on a day of gentle cross- wind I noticed out of the corner of my eye a little plop in a back eddy and mentally filed this as evidence that another fish was moving and decided to cast to it next, when suddenly I realised that my little fly had been blown off course at the last moment of the cast into the eddy and that the plop was a fish! The time for this to register delayed the tightening more than somewhat, but the fish was still well hooked. I suspect that the smallness of the fly slowed the rapid rejection we are used to in loch fishing in these parts, where we strike at the boil or lose fish.

On days of upstream wind (usually easterly) the tactic still works, except that you fish upstream and feel like a chalkstream angler, though the wild hills, heather, sheep and highland cattle don't quite fit. Conventional down-and-across swimming of the fly doesn't seem to work, and bigger flies are ignored or at the best provoke swirls but no takes.

Thus a great deal of standard salmon wisdom — slow strike and all — can be ignored because conditions are so different from those on classic rivers. In Lilliput, concealment, careful casting and non-classic tactics are essential.

The skittering fly tactic seems to be an extension of the irritation principle which can work well on both river and loch. The fish is probably annoyed into swatting the busy little, just sub-surface fly, usually after several workings of the fly over its head in the shallow pool. For the first time in my fishing life I felt confident of taking a fish within minutes of starting, provided I kept low and well back. Once a fish had been landed I moved off to another part of the river, resting the pool after the disturbance. Sometimes ten minutes was enough, but half an hour was better.

I doubt if this tactic will work in bigger streams with deeper pools, but with a steady trickle of fish moving into the river from late July it certainly worked that season. In those larger spate rivers the sinking line and microfly techniques described by Peter Smith in the June 1987 and August 1988 issues of Trout & Salmon would probably work better. However, I much prefer if I can to raise fish to the surface by deception, and in small and shallow pools the skittering small fly does just that. I wonder if a riffling hitch would improve matters even further?

And the flies? I doubt if the pattern matters very much, except that the fish seemed to prefer a fly with some flash in it. My best flies were Silver Stoat's Tail with a rich blue hackle (which makes a most attractive loch fly as well) and Peter Ross, but a late challenger was a seatrout fly given to me by my brother, who fishes the Girvan and the rivers of the south-west of Scotland, the Guinea-fowl and Silver, which has no tail, a ribbed silver body, and well marked natural guineafowl fibres wrapped round as a head hackle.

Most of my fish were typical summer fish from 5 to $9^1/2$ lbs, with a few of 8 lbs, but the holding power of trout hooks, single or double, was made clear by the fact that I lost only one fish that summer and it happened within seconds of tightening into it, the fly coming away intact. If a salmon did not rise to one of these three flies (fished singly, of course) it would at some time come at one of the others, but I am sure that many other flies would work just as well with this method, including a similar sized hairwing Blue Charm, another favourite of mine. All, of course, will take seatrout in a normal season.

No doubt this method, if I can call it that, has been used many times in the past, for there is nothing much that is new in fishing, but for those faced with a small river in low-water conditions and with the knowledge that salmon, stale or otherwise, are in the shallow pools, this is a tactic that can work. But keep well back, use a longish leader, bear manfully the agony of kneeling on hard boulders, and pray (you are in the right position) that yet another theory of salmon fishing is not about to be blown away by the most fascinatingly unpredictable of our game fish.

Chapter 7

JUST as there is a distinctive style of boat fishing in the Outer Hebrides, where the angler sits on a fishing seat (more often a plank of wood!) at the stern and the gillie gently lets the boat down stern first so that the lie can be fished without disturbance, and a taking fish can be followed with ease as the boat is already pointing out into the loch, so we have always had to adapt our techniques to waters sometimes wilder than anywhere else in Britain.

This new-to-me tactic went straight into the diary, one of my latest entries, simply because it represented an elegant, though somewhat alarming solution to what would otherwise have been impossible fishing conditions. Above all, it produced fish where nothing else could have worked, and that is its justification.

If nothing else, it proves that in angling we should always be looking to overcome difficulties in this positive way rather than throwing in our hand because "it hasn't been done before". This one probably has, but I and others had never heard of it before.

Provided that safety is never compromised by such a technique (and this one seems to cover every eventuality) it is well worth a trial in the right (previously wrong) conditions!

The Hebridean rope trick
A minor tactic for loch fishing

Recently I enjoyed a very happy day's fishing in the wild west of Lewis and, as always in fishing new waters, learned something more about our craft. At least, it began as a happy experience, then became positively alarming, and finally ended in great satisfaction after the one nightmarish moment of the day had faded away.

My kind host and his estate manager, Graeme Sinclair, took me on a pleasant two-mile walk to a remote and paradisally beautiful loch which, however, was suffering like everywhere else in these islands that season from a six-week drought. (Do not believe all you see in TV weather forecasts for the Western Isles. Some of us believe that the black blobs indicating rain are automatically inserted on the mistaken assumption that it always rains here.) It was a lovely day for walking, but not for fishing — glaring sun, a brisk to strong north-east wind, and an absence of fresh water to stir up the fish.

Despite all this we had an enjoyable morning session, raising sea trout which tended to short-rise, explicable in the conditions. Then we settled down for lunch on a long, smooth, sandy beach at the east end of the loch where the waves were slightly smaller and we had some protection from the wind. As my up-to-then kind and considerate host finished his sandwiches I heard him say to Graeme: "I think I'll fish from the bank for a bit. I suggest you hang Eddie Young out at the end of a rope for an hour."

Was I meant to hear this? I mentally reviewed my sins of the morning. My casting was not all that bad, surely? How could two people who had demonstrated such courtesy and consideration suddenly turn murderous? Was there no respect for the law in these parts? But it was the Wild West, after all! Yet the landscape was completely treeless. They must have some fiendish substitute. I began to edge away.

But Graeme reassured me with a brief description of my fate. Instead of swinging on a gibbet I was to experience what for me was a completely new tactic for loch fishing designed for days of high wind such as this.

I was placed on the fishing plank at the stern of the boat, with both oars inboard, then Graeme let out the boat on a long rope fixed to the bows so that I faced downwind and began fishing in exactly the same way as if someone was controlling the boat with the oars. Graeme skilfully moved the boat along the water parallel with the beach letting out the rope a little more before moving the boat back to its starting point. I was able to fish stern first, Hebridean fashion, but without anyone at the oars (who would rapidly have become exhausted in battling to hold the boat in the wind), and without the possibility of oar-splash alarming the fish. Such was the smooth efficiency with which Graeme controlled affairs that I could concentrate on fishing, undisturbed by anything extraneous, yet guided by a gentle call, carried down the wind: "Fish right, two o'clock". I was happy to be reminded that the old but highly effective Army system of indicating targets to even the most dim-witted still flourished.

I caught several sea trout, including a splendid four-pounder (on the always reliable Donegal Blue) which I netted once Graeme had pulled the boat into quieter waters. In accordance with the enlightened policy of the

Shipton Pool, River Blackwater, Lewis.

A rare springer, 13 lbs. (R. J. Macleod)

Loch Ulladale, Harris.

The author with a 12 pounder, Lacasdale Lochs, Harris.

estate it was returned, as all the others had been, to help build up a good stock of fish for future seasons. I had played the fish hard in order to bring it in quickly without exhausting it, and Graeme and I had the pleasure of seeing a lovely fish shoot off into the depths immediately it was gently returned. We both felt rather good about that.

Later the three of us discussed the tactic in detail. Of course, there is nothing absolutely new in fishing, and the tactic is used in some of the larger mainland salmon rivers for fishing awkward pools, but its application to loch fishing was new to me. It should be used only in high winds, otherwise the fish could be disturbed by the rope (and there is no point in using the tactic in low winds anyway!). It is not harling (or even, perish the thought, otter-boarding!) as the angler is fly-fishing in exactly the same way as he would if he were being gillied. The operator needs to be skilful in judging distance and in knowing how to avoid letting the boat go over known lies — it is pulled in, moved along, then let out again — and it is important to have the oars inboard in case the operator slips and lets the rope go! A smooth beach is ideal, but even with that it is unwise for the operator to wrap the rope round his person as a trip or stumble could have him hauled into the water like a failed water-skier.

This tactic, therefore, will not work everywhere, but given the right location it could save the day when a big wind gets up and normal boat fishing becomes uncomfortable or even dangerous.

I have now bought a coil of good stout rope. All I have to do is to persuade my usual boat-fishing companions to be hung out on a rope for an hour. I will, however, put it more tactfully.

Chapter 8

WE all have our heroes from the past, including angling ones. They serve as both example and inspiration to us in the present, but only if they have in their lives avoided the trap of dogmatism. Interestingly, the best anglers of the recent past that I have known have scrupulously avoided laying down the law. That, as I have mentioned earlier, has been left to their disciples, who often misunderstood what the master had to say, then worked hard to impose it on the rest of us.

Fortunately this has not happened with the subject of the following portrait, for he was the most modest of men despite having accumulated a great hoard of the best kind of angling wisdom and experience. Apart from the odd article, he wrote nothing about his favourite sport, to all our loss, despite the fact that he wrote with equal facility in Gaelic and English. He is in this a representative figure, for there are many anglers who could leave us the benefit of a lifetime's intelligent angling but who were too modest to write a book about it.

What follows is both an inadequate tribute to the greatest of them and an attempt to pass on something of his example to those who never knew him.

He figures largely in my diary, for even in casual discussion he would drop tentative hints of the best places to fish and the tactics to go with them. After such encounters I would rush back to get it all down on paper, for I knew that I had been in the presence of the best kind of tradition bearer and that something of what he represented had to be preserved in some manner for posterity.

In a great tradition
A Hebridean angler

He was sadly lost to us some years ago, fishing almost to the last. Despite the passage of time some of us still look over our shoulder for reassurance from one we always turned to in time of angling need, to that archetypal figure of our sport, not himself a Hebridean but one who, like some of us, became quickly naturalised, that very great man in every sense of the word, the sometime Depute Rector of The Nicolson Institute, scholar, angler and gentleman, Alec Urquhart. Those who come after him, residents of the Western Isles and our fishing visitors alike, can learn much about angling in these parts from what he has left behind. Above all, he was an example to all anglers everywhere of how to live and how to fish.

At every gathering of anglers during the season or at winter fly-tying sessions his name invariably comes up linked with some illustrative anecdote, with sound advice delivered with his characteristic abrupt kindness and always with a true fisher's concern that you, the listener, should catch fish and enjoy yourself. When I think of that wise and genial presence I see him linked to an illustrious past, to the great tradition of our gloriously absorbing sport, going back in this country as far as the first printed advice to anglers, contained in "The Boke of St Albans" of 1496, entitled "A Treatyse of Fysshynge with an Angle", itself probably written even earlier. "A Treatyse" is usually attributed (probably wrongly) to a prioress, Dame Juliana Berners or Barnes, who managed to run a convent and do a lot of fishing in her spare time, thus establishing another tradition, that of the keen female angler who tends to outfish the male.

The link with holiness is thus early forged (for anglers have always had to be defensive about their sport). It was a seventeenth-century Frenchman, Martial Gujet, who first uttered the notorious libel (later attributed to Dr Johnson but nowhere found in his writings or in his reported utterances) that angling consisted of a line with a worm at one end and a fool at the other. Even today, even though they have some of the finest fly-fishers in the world, the unenlightened among the French refer to idiots as "capable de pecher a la ligne".

So the Treatyse says of the angler (and here logic is stretched to much the same extent as the angler's honesty in describing the one that got away: "Also who soo woll use the game of anglynge; he must rise erly, whyche thyng is prouffytable to men in this wyse, That is to wyte; mooste to the heele of his Soule, For it shall cause hym to be hole. Also to the encrease of his goodys. For it shall make him ryche".

I know few anglers rich in the monetary sense but I do know many rich in other ways, as Alec Urqhart was, and none who delighted more in everything connected with his sport. I see him more accurately in the words of the most famous of angling writers, Izaac Walton, writing in similar defence of angling in "The Compleat Angler" (1653) by linking it with the acknowledged saintliness of a sixteenth-century Dean of St Paul's, Dr Alexander Nowell, cleric, scholar and dedicated angler:

"I say this good man was a dear lover and constant practiser of angling as any age can produce, and his custom was to spend, beside his fixed hours of prayer .... a tenth part of his time in angling and .... to bestow a tenth part of his revenue, and usually all his fish, amongst the poor .... and, at his return to his house, would praise God he had spent the day free from worldly trouble, both harmlessly and in a recreation that became a churchman".

Alec would have said Amen to that. As one who also appreciated the comic in angling he would also have relished the story told by the seventeenth-century theologian, Andrew Fuller, of how Dr Nowell accidently invented something of benefit to us all. Apparently the good man was quietly fishing one day at Battersea during the reign of Queen Mary (of sanguinary memory) when a messenger came to warn him that he was on the monarch's next hit list for the fires at Smithfield. Before catching a fast boat to the Continent he sensibly buried the stone bottle containing his lunchtime ale in a rabbit hole. When Elizabeth came to the throne Dr Nowell returned to London, went fishing as soon as possible, found the correct rabbit hole (anglers are wonderfully exact observers of nature when it suits them), pulled out the bottle, which uncorked with a satisfying pop: "Yet no bottle but rather a gun, for such was the sound at the opening thereof," said Nowell. This well preserved pint inspired Fuller to observe: "To this trifling circumstance is believed to have been the origin of bottle beer in England".

Any such link between angling and drink is, of course, exaggerated and is part of the myth current among non-anglers. There is, of course, no truth in the well known doggerel verse:

"*Behold the angler!*
He riseth early in the morning
And awakeneth the whole household.
Mighty are his preparations.
He returneth when the day is far spent
Smelling of strong drink
And the truth is not in him."

A wiser and more sensible use of the cratur was once explained to me by Alec, a man of moderation in everything but fishing. It was a wild Saturday with a force 10 gale blowing when a friend phoned to say that he had been given tickets for Loch an Ois and asked if I would like to join him. I replied that only a raving lunatic would go fishing on a day like that — and told him to pick me up in half an hour!

When we arrived at the loch it was quite unfishable from the boat; so we fished from the up-wind bank. By great good fortune (which often favours the brave and insane angler) while I was sheltering below a peat bank and letting my flies be carried out into the billows the Butcher on the bob was attacked by a salmon (which was probably also taking shelter). As I was landing it, out of the storm appeared the giant figure of Alec, also carrying a salmon. He had been there since early morning with his son and had not been able to use his boat either. He had at last decided to call it a day. Together we tramped over the moor, laden with oars, tackle and two very unlucky salmon. I found it difficult to keep up with someone considerably older than I, and one whose moor legs were embarrassingly stronger than mine. In the howling storm he loomed over me like some latter-day King Lear on the blasted heath while I, soaked to the skin and puffing hard, stumbled behind like his Fool.

When we reached our cars he turned to me with a quizzical smile and, looking down at me, delivered himself of one of his tersely formal utterances, instantly memorable: "I am going home to have a hot bath. Beside the bath will be one single good dram to restore my constitution. It is on days like this, Mr Young, that you realise why we invented whisky."

His very age linked him to the traditions of the past in surprising ways. I once mentioned to him that I had just read Osgood Mackenzie's "A Hundred Years in the Highlands". To my astonishment Alec said that he well remembered the creator of the Inverewe gardens from the days when he himself was a schoolboy in Gairloch. He summed up the man with typical succinctness — "Fearful old snob" — but there was a twinkle in his eye when he told me the story of how in those days Osgood Mackenzie used to pass on his old tweeds to his head keeper. Alec was short-sighted even in those days, and in a deferential society he took no chances when a figure clad in familiar tweeds came into slightly blurred view and so gave the salute expected by lairds but not by head keepers. As a result he frequently saluted the wrong man and, in consequence, gained the good opinion of the head keeper as a particularly polite boy and was given permission to fish the best spots, a privilege denied to his more keen-sighted schoolfellows.

In a fascinating article he wrote for the Gaelic magazine "Gairm" Alec described these early angling days and how he served his apprenticeship on the little burns before moving on to the lochs and rivers. He also stressed how wholly beneficial a day's fishing can be for anyone under pressure at work in bringing one back to health and sanity — a tradition (and an excuse) — long established in angling literature. But with his usual sense of fun he pointed out the disadvantages to others: "If he does become hooked, there is no word or thought for anything else; the crops are not planted, the peats are not cut, the children cry and the wife becomes a widow . . . but how sweet the sleep is, how interesting the night spent dreaming of lochs still to be fished and of big trout still to be caught".

We used to talk about that remarkable man, the Reverend George Henry Hely-Hutchinson, who wrote the best of all books on fishing in Lewis and Harris, and one of the most enjoyable angling books of all time, 'Reminiscences of The Lews, or Twenty Years of Wild Sport in the Hebrides", published in 1873 under the nom de plume of "Sixty-One". He and Alec had much in common. "Sixty-One" too was an enthusiast, a really keen angler who would fish all day and all night if necessary and who ironically so far succeeded in popularising angling and shooting here that his success led to the leases rising in value until he could not afford to fish here any more. It was then that he wrote his book, which must be read by anyone who fishes in these waters, partly for the good advice it gives but mainly because it is written with such gusto that it becomes a delight to angler and non-angler alike.

It was Alec who told me something not recorded elsewhere, that old people in the Lochganvich area of Lewis still referred to "Sixty-One" as "am ministear cam", for he had only one eye. One Christmas, an old friend sent me a present of a little book on fly-dressing, published in England in 1836 and discovered in an Edinburgh antiquarian bookshop. When I found the original owner's name written on the fly-leaf, "Hy Hutchinson", I rushed to consult Alec. We knew there was a connection with St Peter's Church, Stornoway, as "Sixty-One" fished with his great friend, George Shipton, the then incumbent (the "Shippy" of the book and after whom the Shipton Pool on the Garynahine Blackwater is named). Hely -Hutchinson often helped Shipton with his duties — possibly so that they could go off fishing the earlier — and when I looked up the church register of baptisms and marriages there were dozens of Hely-Hutchinson signatures. The writing was the same! Alec was as delighted as I.

In my own fishing diary Alec's name keeps appearing. He never volunteered advice in case he might be thought patronising, but when asked for help he was generous with his time, accurate in his information and always worth listening to.

"Use a very large Black Pennell on a rough day on Loch an Ois" —this accompanied with the gift of an example. " Try a Mallard and Green for sea trout in September."

" A Wormfly fished in the late evening calm can be deadly." " An ordinary trout Butcher in suitable sizes will take salmon fished either on the bob or tail." "Don't neglect the worm. A real Gorgon''s head of worms on your hook will interest any salmon." (Alec was no purist, though he came to prefer fly-fishing.) "When you are moor-walking, start at the same pace as you mean to finish."

In this way he helped to put me on the right road to adjusting myself to Hebridean conditions, in angling as in our joint profession. Following the precept of Lord Grey of Fallodon his advice did not contain the words "always" or "never", for he was too wise to believe that angling could be reduced to an exact science.

He always kept himself fit, for he knew that angling could be an exhausting business in our wild places, and it was his invariable habit to take a Sunday afternoon stroll with his dog in the Lews Castle Grounds in Stornoway, usually accompanied by that other fine angler, Dugald McLarty. These two never actually strolled. The first time I encountered them on one of their Sabbath training spins I was hard put to keep up with the blistering pace set by these elderly gentlemen. Alec's wee dog was, without doubt, the fittest terrier in Lewis. It is said of Alec that in his eighties he once walked to Loch Langavat in the centre of Lewis, discovered that he had forgotten his reel, walked back to the road, drove home to pick it up, walked again to the loch — and promptly caught a salmon.

Looking back on that fine man and fine angler I realise that the example he set in his chosen recreation was as great as the example he set in his chosen profession, and that is tribute enough. Like the other outstanding figures of the past in that great tradition, he has left us a legacy, a treasury of stories told of him which inspire, encourage and instruct those who follow, giving an added significance to the motto of The Nicolson Institute (I still hear his voice: "Always *The* Nicolson Institute, Mr Young.") which he served with such distinction for so long: "Sequamur" —" Let us follow".

He stands in that great tradition, and I am sure that Dame Juliana, Dr Nowell, Walton and "Sixty-One" have welcomed him to it. As we continue to fish his old haunts we are touched by the presence beside us of that same gruff and friendly spirit that many of us enjoyed for so long.

Let the last words be those of another great angler in that same tradition, T C Kingsmill Moore, Irish judge and author of one of the greatest classics of angling literature, "A Man May Fish". When I fish where Alec used to fish, the second verse of Kingsmill Moore's "Requiescam" is never far from my thoughts, knowing that Alec Urquhart and "Sixty-One" are not far away, wincing perhaps at my bad casting but nodding approval when for once I get things right:

"*Stay not, stranger, passing by.*
For decorous lament or sigh
Where I rest beside you.
Go, my brother, cast your line,
With a craft that once was mine
And good luck betide you."

Chapter 9

GAME fishing as a sport and recreation came to the Western Isles as to many parts of the Highlands as a direct result of the expansion of transport facilities in Victorian times when the railways opened up almost every part of the mainland. The trains linked with ships and ferries to bring the islands within reach even of anglers from the South of England, and by the middle of the century they had reached the Western Isles in small but increasing numbers.

Some of these travellers went back and immediately wrote books about their fishing and their adventures, for to travel to the Islands of the Blessed (and return safely) was noteworthy. There is an attractive innocence about their writings which still holds us today, and their personal example of keen enthusiasm rubbed off on their keepers and gillies who hitherto had to spend too much of their time in subsistence agriculture to be able to take up angling purely as a sport. We owe the best of these visitors much, just as they willingly acknowledged how much they were indebted to the fine men who taught them how to cope with a wilder landscape than they were used to.

Obviously they all kept diaries, just as we all should, for the diary and the game book have one main purpose: to improve our knowledge so that, in future days, we can get even more enjoyment out of our sport.

When I first came to the Western Isles I read every book I could find on fishing here, carefully noting the details in the diary. I learned a lot, and am still learning. Further acquaintance with this very mixed bunch of authors has only increased the debt and lessened the pain of successive close seasons. Newcomers have these delights ahead of them.

Aliens and angling

Once upon a time I had dealings with an incomer to these parts who, with soulless determination, decided that he would absorb what he thought was the culture of the islands to such a degree that he would make himself more Hebridean than the Hebrideans and thus be able to pontificate to other incomers on how they should behave. He became an Authority. He had, of course, absolutely no sense of humour — he hadn't noticed its essential place in the culture of the islands — and in consequence became a source of much merriment to all of us.

One day, having paid him an official visit, I filled in the usual awkward conversational silence so typical of such encounters by announcing brightly that I had just enough time for a couple of hours fishing before getting ready for a meeting I had to attend that evening.

"What sort of fishing?" he enquired coldly, implying that I was almost certainly some kind of moral desperado. "Loch fishing from the bank, with this," I replied, producing my trusty four-piece fly rod which, hidden in its plastic tube masqueraded as a map roll or surveyor's device, thus preserving my cover on such visits.

"Fly-fishing", declared the Authority firmly, "is alien to the culture of the Western Isles. It was imposed by upper-class incomers."

Even by his standards and reputation this was rich, and there was a moment's silence while I struggled with a fit of the giggles, happily repressed, before enquiring sweetly what kinds of fishing were truly "ethnic".

"Worming and spinning", he replied unhesitatingly.

"You mean, using a French spinning reel, a Swedish Toby lure and German nylon monofilament?" enquired I with Socratic innocence.

He humphed, turning abruptly away from the facts as from reality, giving me no chance to remind him that everything was "alien" when first introduced anywhere, even himself, along with his beliefs and prejudices. But he had gone by then, impenetrably armoured in the righteousness of the deeply silly.

I have fished by almost every legal method in my time (and in my unregenerate youth by a few doubtful ones) and never regarded any technique as "alien". Had I missed something?

My first beginning was catching perch with worm and float, then flicking a small worm into moorland burns where they widened into little pools, followed by the upstream worm on rivers (there is no more delicate or skilful fishing technique, and I sometimes got it right), the upstream stonefly nymph, the upstream and downstream wet fly, the dry fly. the spinning of the natural minnow and the unnatural spoon. . . All methods are there for those who prefer them, without prejudice or silly distinctions based on outdated snobberies. I used them all, but eventually simplified them down, especially in loch fishing to which I came rather late, to fly-fishing, because I get most fun out of it. No-one of higher social status taught me. My mentors when I was small were Lanarkshire steelworkers and miners, glad to be out of the melting shop or wet seam into the open air, yet never too impatient to stop fishing and put me on the right lines while being wonderfully generous with bits of tackle. I still remember them with gratitude.

Of course, my Authority didn't fish at all and never had: most dogmatic people have no experience of what they are laying down the law about, and facts do get in the way of blind prejudice; but the incident bothered me, for again and again I have run into those who would like to fish with the fly but tell me that it is too difficult or, amazingly in this day and age, "Fly-fishing is not for the likes of us".

The answer to this negative attitude, as with many others, lies in the past. All that we loosely call our " culture" comes from somewhere. We adapt it, modify it, give it our own personal stamp and sometimes re-export it — rather like the acceptance of Christianity by the peoples of these western parts and the development of the Celtic Church, eventually leading to that Church's missionary drive into Europe in the Dark Ages, re-exporting the Faith — a movement which played such a great part in civilizing the continent. As with great things, so with small. Fly-fishing is very old, recorded as far back as Aelian (c 170 - 235 AD), and it came into Scotland early. I like to think that William Wallace's first brush with the English soldiers over his fishing near Lanark was an interruption to his casting a fly, in the great tradition of the upper part of Clydesdale.

The popularising of angling, fly and spinning, came indeed from outside. The great central text is, of course, the marvellous "Reminiscences of The Lews, Twenty Years of Wild Sport in the Hebrides", by "Sixty-One", the Reverend George Henry HelyHutchinson, of whom I have written earlier and who lived here between 1850 and 1870, basing himself on Aline and Soval Lodges. Anyone interested in the nineteenth century in Lewis and Harris should read it, for its author loved the island and its people deeply (despite a feelingly written chapter on "Lewis Climate and Midges"). There is nothing more poignant in angling literature than his farewell when, growing old and less able to walk the moor, and unable to pay the increased rental for his shootings and fishings, he was obliged to return to the mainland.

"Sixty-One" must have had a great influence on the good side. He seems to have been friendly with everyone in all levels of society, and very appreciative of the skills and sometimes courage of those he employed. I have already mentioned his great friend, Shipton, the incumbent of St Peter's, commemorated in the Shipton pool on the Garynahine Blackwater where he caught salmon despite thrashing the water with huge flies and almost invariably breaking his specially strengthened rods.

Even at that date "Sixty-One" speaks of the expertise of Lewismen with a fly rod. Sir James Matheson's piper, Thomas McKay, "would send his fly as far as any one I ever saw", and the author later tells us "that about one of the best and most successful (anglers) I ever saw in my life , Sir James Matheson's piper, never fished a loch but from the shore, and always laughed at me and my boat, and nobody knows the quantity of fish he has killed in his life". Any loch fly-fisher will tell you how difficult it is to take a salmon by casting from the shore as this normally requires fishing into or at least close to the wind (since salmon tend to lie on a lee shore) with your flies moving from deep to shallow instead of from shallow to deep, which last the fish prefer. Thomas McKay must have been a world-class caster. It seems reasonable to believe that there were many others in Lewis and Harris at that time who were at least more than competent with a fly rod.

Captain J T Newall (" late Indian Staff Corps", as he describes himself), author of the imperially titled "Scottish Moors and Indian Jungles", published in 1889, came to Scaliscro in 1880. He was a remarkable man: having badly injured his spine in a riding accident in India so that he could no longer walk, he designed a kind of litter in which he was carried over the moors by four men and from which he shot both game birds and deer. He also fished his favourite Loch an Fhir Mhaoil from a chair in the boat, and managed to fish the Grimersta and the Blackwater as well. He had the greatest admiration for his Lewis and Harris stalkers, gillies and carriers, especially the man on the front poles of the litter who had to get used to shot whistling past his ears!

The good tradition was carried on by John Bickerdyke, author of "Days in Thule" (1894), who took Gress Lodge (disguised as "Gheira" in the book) sometime in the 1890's. A very keen fly-fisher, he invented the concept of "Salmo Irritans", a fish that won't take, and devised a new hook on which to dress flies specifically to deal with the problem. It's interesting to note that the famous modern authority on salmon and seatrout fishing, Hugh Falkus, has revived the classification under the name of a "Hamlet" fish, based on the awful misinterpretation of the hero's state of mind given world -wide currency by the introduction to Sir Laurence Olivier's film of the play, and uttered in a portentously daft tone by the narrator: "This is the tragedy of a man who could not make up his mind", thus reducing one of the world's greatest plays to the study of a weak-minded ditherer. The "Sixty- One" tradition still lived, for Donald, the head-keeper was a good fly-fisher and Sandy, the second keeper "had done service with "Sixty-Three" (clearly a mistake in arithmetic).

The man who seems to have established the bad tradition, of the offensive incomer, was C. V. A. Peel, author of "Wild Sport in the Outer Hebrides" (1901). He appears to have been something of a colonialist, regarding the Western Isles as a colony populated by restive "natives" — he was also the author of "Somaliland" — and certainly did not set out to make himself agreeable to anyone north of the Border. He didn't like Scotsmen in general: ". . . the Scotsman whose motto is always, 'Keep the Sabbath and everything else you can lay your hands on'," and his blanket condemnation of the "natives" has become a classic of its kind: "They were especially insolent and troublesome in Benbecula and Barra. Taking them as a whole, the crofters are an ignorant lot of creatures, and the less said about them the better". The feeling that we are dealing with a cartoon character from a back issue of "Punch" is strengthened by an unbelievable photograph of the author, captioned "Ready for the Fray", festooned with creel, rod, net and impedimenta, with his waders hanging round his neck, and looking for all the world, with moustache, flashing teeth and cigarette, like the characters once played by the film actor, Terry Thomas, on a bad day. Apart from shooting at everything that moved he was a fly-fisher, and probably created the wrong associations for the craft in the minds of some of the "natives".

Perhaps the best known of our angling visitors was Cecil Braithwaite, who was closely associated with the Grimersta during the early part of this century, whose books include "Fishing Vignettes", "Fishing Here and There" and (my candidate for the most innocently twee title of any book on country sports) "Happy Days with Rod, Gun and Bat" (for he was also a cricketer). This nice man was, however, a product of his age, and his unconscious condescension, though kindly meant, to the "natives" perfectly caught the flavour of the period and reinforced the myth of fly-fishing being something confined to the "right" people. In one book there is a solemn photograph of six people, captioned "Major JH and Mrs Knox", the other four human beings being merely gillies. In another, the head keeper of Grimersta is allowed to write two chapters on his own recollections of the Grimersta. He writes in clear and polished English, in stark contrast with Braithwaite's clumsy prose, and the beauty of it is that Cecil doesn't notice!

It is now easy to see how the myth about fly-fishing became current in these parts, inspiring my Authority in his bigoted balderdash , because it became associated with some (by no means all) visitors and incomers whose social attitudes were entirely different from those they came among. Largely unconscious condescension (not entirely absent even today) did a great deal of damage. Happily, the best of them, from "Sixty-One" onwards, were welcomed for what they were as human beings, and they responded warmly and positively. In this tradition, the islanders picked up what was worth learning from these visitors and discarded what was not. Among the good things was fly-fishing, and some of the best fly-fishers I have ever known (an increasing number) are from these parts, casting their flies with a skill and a grace which seem directly descended from Thomas McKay, Sir James Matheson's piper, and many more unrecorded.

The Authority has long since taken his prejudices elsewhere, along with his negative approach to the good things of life. There is a moral here: good things are good in themselves and not to be judged in relation to real or imagined bad things. Wise fishermen, like wise men and women everywhere, are eclectic in their tastes — we select what gives us the most harmless enjoyment in our richly satisfying obsession, go out and about in all weathers, close to nature and at peace with the world, secure in the knowledge that we follow a good and great tradition. And our latter-day visitors feel the same!

Chapter 10

ANGLERS are incurable optimists and very rapidly excise the memory of bad and unproductive days from the memory. Theirs is the attitude of the Revd Charles Kingsley:
"I'm off at eight tomorrow morn,
  To bring *such* fishes back!"

Despite too many diary entries describing failure (briefly detailed) there are others of some length which deserve to be read aloud to triumphalistic background music. That's when we get it all right, when by a combination of good luck and the right conditions, with just a tiny little bit of skill, we have a good day.

But some days are not just good but special. Those are the rare occasions when the heavens seem to open and blessings, not downpours of rain, are undeservedly showered on us. At such times and afterwards anglers become uncharacteristically inarticulate as they attempt to convey the uncanny magic of such a day. On such occasions we are touched by something almost mystical and find it very difficult to shrug off.

Anyone who has had such a day knows what I mean; others are cut off from the mystery simply by never having experienced it. I am firmly of the belief that such days, though very rare, offer themselves more often to anglers in these parts than elsewhere and constitute (though we are usually too embarrassed to speak about them openly) an essential part of the deepest and most lasting delights of an angling life. Wordsworth knew of them and wrote about them, but of course he was himself a keen angler and thus a sharer in our mysteries.

Once in a lifetime

What makes a perfect day's fishing? It comes seldom, if at all, but when it does its glory is enhanced by the memory of blank, fishless, desperate days, which may have their own masochistic attraction for some but are not to be dwelt upon at length.

The perfect day is not simply a matter of catching fish, though that is essential — I deplore the sentimentalists' claim that they go fishing purely for the sound of rushing waters and the twittering of birds (Why don't they leave their rods behind?) — but it is true that the perfection lies in much more than a good basket.

I have had one perfect day, though a few others have come close, and it may be that I have had my life's ration, but I cannot complain if I don't have another. Analysing why it was so enjoyable is less easy, but the analysis of life's pleasures often leads to their greater enjoyment, especially in fishing, where we are always seeking rational justification for our splendidly irrational obsession. "The Compleat Angler" is full of it.

Expectation is part of it. The days of preparation, the careful checking of gear, tackle and trim, the doubts over the weather-forecaster's confident predictions (often producing much hollow laughter in these latitudes) all build up to the glorious moment of release from the responsibilities and constraints of the workaday world and we enter, however briefly, a timeless and enchanted land. Expectation is heightened the more if we are to fish new and unexplored waters, especially if they promise much. The first sight of a far loch, a glint of sun on water, lengthens the stride and etches the scene into the memory.

Years ago Roddy and I were given permission to fish a little jewel of a loch, several miles over moor and hill in one of the remotest corners of these islands. After a long, hot, dry summer it was now mid-August and for three days the blessed rains had come at last, though they still had some work to do before the lochs filled up again and the little burns ran bank-high.

On Friday night it rained heavily and steadily. I know, because I heard it. Normally I sleep like a log but I always have difficulty in sleeping before an expedition of this kind. When the alarm-clock rang I moved out of bed with a speed and sense of purpose I seldom show on other, more mundane mornings.

The fishing clothes, those old, comfortable symbols of liberation from the humdrum were slipped on silently. The household slept on. A good solid breakfast, a final check of all equipment, food and drink into the boot of the car, then the great moment when the car purred off along silent streets arriving at Roddy's house in perfect time for a 6.45 am start. The rain still fell, lighter now, as I virtuously contemplated my compliance with the adjuration in 1st Kings, Chapter 18, Verse 41: "Get thee up, eat and drink; for there is a sound of abundance of rain".

When I arrived at Roddy's house no lights showed. This was odd. Roddy sleeps even less than I do before such expeditions. Deciding that such a fall from grace deserved immediate rebuke I battered at his door knocker. Lazy blighter, holding us up. Then I looked at my watch — 5.45 am!

I returned at the proper time, suitably chastened, endured Roddy's mirth, then at last we were off south, experiencing that special quality of exhilaration which goes with the knowledge that we had a full day's sea trout fishing in wild places ahead of us. The rain began to ease off, but at each turn of the road we saw the burns cascading down hillsides lit by the early-morning sun. It was good to be alive.

We parked the car at the beginning of the rough track which led over the pass through the hills to the loch. Miraculously the rain had stopped altogether, the sun shone , and we felt a very gentle west wind blow on to our left cheeks. No need for hampering waterproofs as we shouldered our packs and swung up the hillside, settling into the steady, economical pace essential for moorland walking. I had stuffed my home-made collapsible salmon net-head into my pack and walked with the aid of the net handle, a five-foot broom handle with fitted screw-ferrule to take the net head at one end and with a rubber buffer at the foot, a useful third leg on rough terrain. Later I was to be very glad of it.

Ignoring for once the received wisdom for moor-walking in these parts — start at the same pace as you intend to finish — we soon found ourselves moving at a faster speed than usual, the adrenalin of expectation pushing us on. When we reached the watershed we providently left two cans of lager under the waterfall as a cooling restorative for the return journey. The track now dropped steeply for two more miles, promising a hard climb on the way back. Not that we worried — then! The hills were still shedding the overnight rain but the sun was warm, the air was fresh from the Atlantic, and as the glen began to open out we saw it at last — a glitter of water in the north. Our pace increased. After losing and finding the loch again and again in the undulations of the track we saw it suddenly open out before us, beautiful in the morning light.

Already a few sea trout made tantalising swirls on the almost flat surface.

The loch was nearly brim-full but the water was quite clear as the run-off from the feeder burns came straight from the rock of the surrounding hills. We tackled up with hasty fingers, at once distracted and driven on by the rings made by rising fish, very clear in the scarcely ruffled waters. No salmon moved.

We decided on light tackle — 5lb or 6lb leaders as long as we could handle and size 12 or 10 sea trout flies. As usual, we had the Donegal Blue on the bob and Harold's Grouse and Claret on the tail. I put a Black Pennell on the dropper.

As Roddy had fished this loch once before and as it was my first visit he insisted on being gillie for the opening half hour. As he very quietly and carefully placed the boat off the mouth of the main feeder burn (the rest of the loch was almost flat calm) I cast my flies over the fringe of the current. On the sixth cast — I counted them — I had a perfect, classic, slow head-and-tail rise to the Donegal Blue and, as if in a dream, I held my hand until the fish rolled over and down. (I seldom achieve that fine quality of restraint.)

It fought like the perfectly fresh $2^1/_2$ lb fish it was, with spectacular leaps and runs that made the reel sing, and I sagged with relief when Roddy expertly netted it in my homemade boat net, now reassembled and doing its job efficiently, unlike the clumsy over-heavy thing which went with the boat.

The whole picture of rise, roll, tighten and fight, searing runs and powerful leaps remains forever imprinted in the memory — the cameo of a perfect day. Of such are the immediate and lasting joys of sea trout fishing in wild places.

Two more sea trout of around $1^1/_2$ lbs followed, then, when I took the oars, everything went quiet and we did little for the rest of the morning.

We had a substantial lunch, devoured at just under indigestion speed before beginning the afternoon's fishing, again in the very lightest of airs. (We should, of course, have had a leisurely and extended lunch as recommended in Victorian and Edwardian accounts of such fishing, but who nowadays can stay to eat when fish are moving.)

And move they did. It only slowly dawned on us that we now had a falling loch which, despite the very light wind, was worth exploiting to the full. The change must have begun soon after we arrived, when the flow of the burns gradually slackened. In such conditions sea trout usually take well.

I decided to deploy my one rowing skill, developed years before in my own small boat when teaching my daughters to fish, of gillying and fishing at the same time. When I have positioned the boat for my partner I move back to the bows and start fishing myself. This involves frequent moves back to the oars to adjust the drift. I usually manage this without falling overboard. It requires, of course, a fairly light wind for this ploy to be successful and you have to be quiet in your movements. It works well for sea trout in these conditions, but you have to take to the oars and gillie properly as you approach the salmon lies near the downwind shore. I haven't the skill of some Irish anglers who fish happily and effectively with an oar tucked under an armpit, at the same time both fishing and controlling the boat with an economy of effort which I can only admire.

So I took over the gillying, and Roddy immediately began to take fish after fish, rapidly overhauling my catch. I reminded him that in this kind of fishing everything depends on the skill of the gillie.

"Absolutely true," said he, "so keep at it," as he raised and hooked another good fish.

The sea trout were clearly fresh-run and soft-mouthed. Despite the most careful handling they often took off on long and exciting runs then, without jumping or being put under anything but the lightest of pressure, simply let the fly drop out of their mouths. How this is done is a recurring mystery in both loch and river. From that experience I resolved to make myself a longer and more forgiving rod for this kind of fishing — an 11 foot carbon fibre one, taking a 6 or 7 line. It and its variations have served me ever since, perfect not only for sea trout but also for our summer salmon, which seldom run large.

The Donegal Blue and Harold's Grouse and Claret took all the fish. The Black Pennell, usually and since the most dependable of loch flies, for once did nothing. We had a few dull spells, enough to keep the fishing interestingly uncertain, and even they were enjoyable in the wild and beautiful surroundings of this wonderful loch. But time, even in Arcadia, moves on inexorably.

I struck a particularly bad patch when I lost three good fish in succession to the firm-take, long-run, release-the-fly trick. The Black Dog, that grinning elemental so well described by Sydney Spencer when he fished these waters settled itself at my end of the boat. Roddy (a purer soul?) was unaffected. I kept on fishing — the only way to beat this particular bogy (apart from checking your hook points, which I did).

It was now very late in the day. Roddy selflessly decided to go ashore to begin preparing the gear for the long trek back to the car while I, selfishly, tried a last drift on my own — no great problem in the gentle zephyr. My tail fly, Harold's Grouse and Claret, was engulfed by a really good fish, first throw. Praying fervently to the Blessed Izaak Walton I tightened, yet half resigned to its coming off like the last three. Only when it at last jumped perilously close to the boat did I realise that I had hooked a salmon, the only one seen in the loch that day. Blessedly (thank you, Izaak) the hook held.

If you ever find yourself in this nerve-stretching predicament, alone in a boat drifting towards a thick weed bed and attached to a show-jumping salmon on a light leader, the only solution I can offer is to bring it upwind of the boat — always good practice — thus letting it help to keep you away from the weeds and exhaust itself in the process. It worked, and eventually I was able to slip my net under a nice summer salmon. The Black Dog fled, whimpering.

The net provided with the boat would have been far too heavy for such single-handed work. Its net ring was, unbelievably, smaller than that of my portable home-made article. Anyone making the journey to fish from a boat on a remote loch would be well advised to make up a net like this — the materials are easily purchased and, even today, remarkably inexpensive. As a bonus you have the third leg on the hill mentioned earlier, ideal for those of mature years and a useful walking aid for anyone.

The day, the perfect day, was nearly over. The thought of a late evening's fishing was tempting, as a nice breeze had risen instead of an uncertain ripple, but we had a long way to go — and the next day was the Sabbath.

We shared out 25 good sea trout and one unexpected salmon, at the same time considering with some apprehension the first two, very steep, at times almost perpendicular miles to the watershed. It was hard slogging with frequent pauses for recovery. Had we caught more, would we have been able to carry them? As we reached the watershed the sky began to darken. The light in these glens fades fast.

We had ten minutes much-needed rest. The lager, deliciously cold from the waterfall, for once did all that its makers claimed for it. Restored in all parts we covered the last two miles downhill at a swinging pace.

As we moved through the pass a great full moon rose majestically over the hills to the east, silhouetting in Landseerian splendour a stag and two hinds high above us on the darkening ridge. Nature was imitating art. It was then that we reflected that all day we had not seen a single human being.

What were the qualities of that perfect day? The expectations were high; the preparations were exciting; the weather was fine; the journey to and from the loch was strenuously exhilarating; the surroundings were wild and beautiful; the fishing was good, yet uncertain enough to keep all our senses alert. All these had their contribution to make, and everything was brought together by the special relationship of two anglers in a boat, each genuinely keen that the other should do well. This last is the essence of enjoyable boat fishing, whether on Hebridean loch or lowland reservoir.

I fell into bed that night, just before midnight, recalling the words of this century's greatest poet, W B Yeats, an Irishman who fished a bit, as he recalled a moment of pure visionary delight, so intense, "That I was blessed and could bless". I knew what he meant.

Perhaps we anglers, odd and irrational breed that we are, are all mystics at heart.

It's a thought.

Spoilt for choice!

September salmon.

The veterans, Fin and Dougal, Loch Carason.

Chapter 11

THIS is a purely personal statement, though I think that much of it should apply to all of us, and it comes appropriately towards the end of this book. Perhaps it will reassure those contemplating retirement; better still it might encourage young anglers in the knowledge that they have taken up an activity which will enrich their whole lives, and with luck will prolong them.

At this stage in one's life the fishing diary has expanded to several volumes. It is sometimes painful to read of past mistakes and foolish errors, as in the records of more famous diarists (Samuel Pepys among the most honest), but we all can learn from these mistakes. Not that the retired angler is a fount of all knowledge because of this: he or she has learned not to make the old mistakes, but most of us are now eagerly committing new ones, and great fun it all is. Omniscient anglers are as tiresome as know-alls in any walk of life, and the only certain wisdom to be expected from fishers of mature years is that they have learned precisely that. Flee from any who haven't.

With this in mind, the retired angler should try to pass on the knowledge of the pleasures and excitements of an angling life to younger folk, and the diaries should have plenty of that kind of entry. I bless those who took the time to do this for me long ago, and I can think of no greater gift to pass on in my turn.

And so it is with an unusually clear conscience that we happily retired anglers can now more frequently hang up, at least in metaphor, that most evocative of notices: "Gone Fishing!"

The retiring angler
or
Happy ever after

I write of "retiring", not in the sense of "shy and...." (which no-one can accuse me of) but of the cessation of normal employment, the consequences of which have been for long the subject of much earnest discussion, innumerable long-winded dissertations, and a spate of books, pamphlets and even magazines devoted to the purpose of telling us how to cope with this so-called traumatic time of life. Of course, if we have lived a full and active life then retirement is more of an opportunity than a problem, and we should not need any of the "counselling" that is often inflicted on our non-fishing friends.

I am not going to tell anglers how to cope with retirement, just make a report after a few years' experience. The news is good. In fishing terms the years of retirement can be the happiest of your life, far better in reality than the romantic remembrances of my own youth of burn fishing in the days when all the world was young. As one of my 87-year-old fishing friends put it to me when he was a mere 80: "In what other sport can you confidently expect that at my age your greatest days may lie in the future?" He then went on to land 23 salmon that summer; and after a major operation one spring he badgered me to escort him on foot to a moorland loch to try out his legs, caught a couple of nice trout, announced himself fit for service, and was soon eagerly pursuing his first summer salmon.

Much conventional wisdom exists on the subject of retirement. All of us know that it is a test of the kind of person you are, or of the kind of person you have become, of the interests you have developed both inside and outside your work, and of your capacity to retain a positive attitude to life together with a flexibility of mind far more important than flexibility of muscle. Retirement, in fact, tells you a lot about yourself, along with the rueful realisation that it's probably a bit late to change now, though it can be done. But happy is the angler, for he possesses that paradoxical essential to full mental health — an all-absorbing irrational obsession which depends on optimism beyond sense and reason, backed up by a positive driving energy. In other words, it helps to be slightly mad if you want to be happily sane. I am fortunate in having the example of older friends to follow, who have the same cast of mind. They consider me but a callow stripling with much to learn. They are right on the last point: like all fishers of whatever age I am, as an old angler of my boyhood put it to me , "aye learnin".

Anyone approaching retirement should read Charles Ritz's monumental "A Fly Fisher's Life" — everyone should read it, anyway — especially the chapter entitled "Health". In it Ritz very sensibly outlines the inevitable physical and mental effects of increasing age and the precautions one should take to ensure a longer and happier fishing life. The revised edition with new material by the author came out in 1972 when Ritz was eighty. He identifies the problems of advancing age as those involving the heart (physical, that is, not romantic) and the weight-bearing skeleton. (Not much left, one thinks.) Other problems, he believes, "are the result of excessive eating, drinking and smoking; sometimes all three". He obviously knew his fishermen. Ritz recommends, from the age of 50, the seeking of sound medical advice on strains and pains from medically qualified osteopaths, and the advantages of regular isometric exercises. As we become older, he claims, we become more nervous (I haven't noticed it yet); therefore we should teach ourselves to relax. We should never eat to excess but always choose a balanced diet and stick to red wine (agreed!) or water. We should all try to walk at least one hour each day. He concludes that the trouble involved in taking care of oneself when young is amply repaid in later years.

All this is good sensible stuff from one who was fanatically keen on fishing — though it all sounds heroically self-restrained from the proprietor of the Ritz in Paris for whom self-indulgence must have been a daily temptation — but Ritz realised that it is difficult to fish well without feeling well, and that the feedback is that if you fish well you will in consequence feel well!

My own experience may be of interest. I foolishly believed that I would have all the time in the world for fishing, living as I do in the middle of marvellous wild brown trout fishing, usually free, and with fairly accessible sea trout and salmon waters. But if you retire with many interests you find they tend to clash occasionally, and fishing can suffer. I also at first tended to become selective, waiting for the best fishing conditions before setting out. This was most unwise, for our weather seems to be beyond the predictive skills of the meteorologists, and in any case some of my most enjoyable and productive expeditions have been on days when fishing seemed plain daft. The simple rule is that fishing comes first — or at least after life-and-death situations (well, some of them). You owe it to yourself to be selfish occasionally. Then you will have all the exercise that Ritz recommends: a walk of one hour a day on dry, flat ground is piddling compared with a day tramping to and from a remote loch or sharing the rowing of a boat in a salmon wave.

Physically I feel as fit as ever, but I take a little longer to recover after prolonged exertion. I keep fit by gardening and, in the winter, by walking, and for years I have put in a few minutes a day during the close season on the old Canadian Air Force exercises.

The secret, if there is one, of being a happily retired angler, lies in a life of purposeful activity which is enjoyable and exciting. One of my older friends, a non angler, told me that the first six months of retirement were dreadful — he simply couldn't get up in the morning — and that was after a hectic business career. Too late he realised that he had no business, and the shock nearly took him off. Now he has each day planned the night before, but he would never have had such problems had he been a fisher.

I read everything I can about fishing. I collect fishing books, especially the truly terrible ones written by engaging enthusiasts of the past whose keenness led them to write lots of cheerful rubbish. I tie a few flies almost daily, most of which go to friends, write a fishing column in one of the great newspapers of the western world, the Stornoway Gazette, which has exiled subscribers in almost every country on the globe, the result of the Clearances and the Hebridean talent for successful settlement throughout the old Empire, and occasionally write for the angling press.

In retirement, as I have said, the mental attitude is of the essence. I know elderly men who behave like schoolboys at the prospect of a day's fishing, even if they have been at it the day before. I am always excited when approaching river or loch, even if I have fished it many times before; and a new one will give me a sleepless night beforehand. If it is an old friend the very fact that I know it well raises all sorts of urgent questions: will that point fish well in this wind and at this time of the season, and should I try that new fly I tied last night? Excitement, reasonably controlled, is all. Lose it, and you might as well take up fretwork.

Years ago, I fell for every new concoction dreamed up by flytying lunatics and published as the surest way of emptying the water of fish. With all the wisdom of long experience I now do exactly the same. I am excited when I tie up the latest Bloggs Bagstrainer, and when I first put it to the test, and I am totally unabashed when it doesn't work. Incidentally, the most deadly boring angler is he who assures you that you *must* use this fly or this method. These grow up from being young bores to becoming old bores, immediately recognisable by their elbow-gripping opening: "What you want to do is......." We have none such in these parts.

I now have a select group of flies in which I have great trust, but I fish them only after I have tried out the experimental ones, for rigidity of mind and attitude is something to be avoided as one gets older. Every so often one of the newcomers actually catches fish and is then promoted to the second rank, the ones I fish after the failure of the new. The reliable ones come out eventually in an attempt to save the day if required. Be open-minded, if necessary bloody-minded, in your attitude to tradition and the way things have "always" been done. That way, you stay young.

Our great advantage over the non-fishing superannuated is that we retain the excitement of youth, the moment when we breast the ridge and see before us the sparkling waters and start to run (honestly!) over the last

Salmon and seatrout from the bank.

Photo by the late F. W. Horrobin. Courtesy of Borve Lodge Estate.

few yards. My older friends still do it, and I can't stop myself. Long may it continue.

And when it is all over? We have the consolations of literature, from Kingsmill Moore's "Requiescam", where the spirit of the departed angler still fishes his beloved waters to John Buchan's more believable (especially if you are a Scot) "Fisher Jamie" who, becoming bored with fishing the heavenly streams, goes in for a bit of poaching:

"*And syne wi' saumon on his back,*
Catch't clean against the Heavenly law,
And Heavenly byliffs on his track,
Gaun linkin' doun some Heavenly shaw."

Disreputable, but there is a touch of the agreeable scoundrel in all good fishers, especially the old ones, no matter how respectable we all are nowadays in our decorous retirement.

Chapter 12
Flies

First are the so-called "traditional" Scottish loch flies, which form the basis of the Hebridean loch fisher's armoury. They have become traditional, even classic, simply because over a long period of time they have proved their value in taking fish. Their other great merit is that they are not just brown trout flies; they attract salmon and sea trout just as well, and frequently better, than conventional salmon flies. Visiting anglers often have difficulty in coming to grips with this crossing of categories.

These traditional trout flies, tied on trout hooks from size 14 to 6, are simply essential. (Salmon irons, singles, doubles or trebles, have their place, but more of that later.)

A second group are the incomers, imported from other parts of the UK or North America, some of which are already well on the way to becoming the traditionals of the future. The wise angler adds them to the fly-box, using them as front-line troops, confident in the knowledge that, if they fail, the veterans probably won't.

The even wiser fisher will continually experiment, sometimes with surprisingly good results, even with the apparently outrageous. Only time will tell if these innovations are what Kingsmill Moore called "Single Speech Hamiltons" or become consistently high-class orators; but almost every season a new and worthwhile fly is added to our lists from modification, innovation or invention, no matter how apparently bizarre. It is unwise to be hidebound by tradition, but it is comforting to know that it is there to be followed if desired.

A third group are the newcomers, a relative term since some are now well established.

A fourth group are those flies usually known as purely salmon flies. They have their place both in loch and river, but it is not an exclusive place.

The following is a list of the four main categories (plus some miscellaneous extras) with dressings given where they might be found useful. Naturally, this is a personal list, but it should cover most fishing circumstances.

1. Traditionals

These are, by definition, too well known to require printed dressings except for possible minor variations in tying. Comments on some of them follow after their listing:

Alexandra, Black Zulu, Blue Zulu, Blae and Black, Butcher (and variations: Gold, Kingfisher, Hardy's), Black Pennell (body of black floss and oval silver rib, or black seal's fur and flat silver rib), Camasunary Killer, Cardinal, Cinnamon and Gold, Dark Mackerel, Greenwell's Glory (along with the Spider and Nymph dressings), Dunkeld, Grouse and Claret, Heather Moth, Invicta, Kate McLaren, Poacher, Worm Fly, Wickham's Fancy.

Two others are essentially trout flies (though someone will surely prove me wrong): Black and Peacock Spider, Brown and Peacock Spider.

Black Pennell, Black Zulu, Blue Zulu and Soldier Palmer are the great bob flies of the islands. Black Pennell is a persistent taker of salmon. Malcolm Greenhalgh, the well known angling writer and scientist (Trout Fisherman, January 1986) spent three weeks trout fishing with his young son in Lewis and Harris in July and found, despite frequent experimental changes of fly, that the Blue Zulu accounted for over 60% of their fish. It also takes many salmon each season. I am personally addicted to the Black Zulu for loch salmon fishing. Even in low winds it can be effective, tied on hooks as small as trout size 10, especially late in the season. Dibbled through the neck of a river pool, usually on a salmon 10 double with a larger fly on the tail, it can work wonders. The Butcher is all-purpose, and a splendid salmon fly, especially the hair-wing version, probably because of its resemblance to the Silver Stoat's Tail. The Soldier Palmer is a great all-season trout fly, and equally good for the other game fish.

Blae and Black can also be fished with profit in Tom Saville's variation: Glo-Brite No 3 tail, oval silver rib, black seal's fur body, black hen hackle, blae wing. The old Scottish variation with a red feather tail (like the Butcher) has also proved itself.

Cardinal was once a great sea trout fly and it has been revived, especially in North Uist where the oval silver ribbed version is effective in brackish water and the gold ribbed in peaty lochs, for trout, sea trout and even salmon.

Cinnamon and Gold is good for trout in small sizes (12 and 14) and for both sea trout and salmon in larger.

Dunkeld works well for all our game fish. Its gold body shows up well in peaty water, and it once brought me a salmon in very thick mist.

Grouse and Claret, an all- season trout fly and very popular in Harris, is equally effective for sea trout and salmon. Charles McLaren refers to it as a good fly to keep off your cast in September lest you hook a salmon and so spoil your sea trout fishing! See Chapter 5 for a wonderfully effective variation.

Invicta is especially good for grilse and always an excellent trout fly. The silver version also works well.

Kate McLaren is reliable in all sizes and a favourite for seatrout and salmon in the Uists. Charles Mc Laren, after whose mother the fly was named by its originator, William Robertson of the long-established Glasgow tackle shop, stresses in the second edition of "The Art of Sea Trout Fishing" that the collar hackle should be of natural hen "so as to work properly in the water". This requirement for a hen hackle of the appropriate colour should also apply to any of the above palmer flies to bring out their full effectiveness, the palmered cock hackle giving the necessary "kick" and the softer, preferably longer, hen hackle creating the illusion of life.

March Brown is always good, but particularly in the spring. March Brown Silver is a good seatrout and salmon fly. I prefer it in its older dressing of hare's lug body ribbed with flat silver, rather than one wholly of silver.

Peter Ross, as is its due, is given a whole chapter to itself (Chapter 6).

Teal, Blue and Silver will take early trout, and then sea trout and salmon throughout the season. Kingsmill Moore found that it worked only for fresh run fish in Ireland. Our fish must have different tastes.

2 Incomers

Ireland:

It must be Celtic affinity, for Irish flies work as well here as in their native land.

Bibio, fished mainly on the bob, with either a red or orange body midsection, is an excellent bob fly for trout, sea trout and salmon throughout the season.

Connemara Black is very good for trout in small sizes and is reliable for sea trout and salmon.

Dabbler in all its versions is a good rough weather fly anywhere on the cast.

Bumbles (Kingsmill Moore) especially the Claret, are good for everything. The Golden Olive Bumble, a superb trout fly, takes salmon as well in these waters.

Donegal Blue is a deeply personal favourite of mine for sea trout and salmon. It can also be very good for brown trout. See Chapter 5.

Goat's Toe and its variations, fished on tail or bob, is becoming increasingly popular for sea trout and salmon and is another of my favourite Irishmen. I find it best dressed with body and rib reversed from the traditional dressing so that the body is peacock herl and the rib red floss, making a much stronger fly. I like the tail of red floss or wool to be rather long and prominent.

Sooty Olive has also many variations. It is an excellent trout fly which fishes well in the middle of a three-fly leader throughout the season.

Wales:
Haul a Gwynt (Sun and Wind) is absurdly simple to tie: black ostrich herl body, folded crow wing, collar hackle of cock pheasant neck feather in front of wing. It works well under all conditions, all through the year and not just in sun and wind. Brown trout take it with complete confidence, probably because it represents many of our little black flies. Fish it on sizes 14 and 12. Although Moc Morgan does not recommend it on larger sizes, it has done well here as big as size 8 in a good wave. Another personal favourite.

Coch a Bonddu (now the established spelling) has been with us a long time and has built up a great reputation as a bob fly.

England:
The Ombudsman (Brian Clarke) requires a whole chapter to itself. See Chapter 4.

North America:
The Muddler Minnow has done the near-impossible of successfully challenging the Blue Elver as the favoured bob fly for salmon fishing on the Grimersta system. It has now spread all over the islands where it not only raises salmon, to be taken on the tail fly, but also takes more than its share itself.

3. Newcomers

The Clan Chief, devised by Captain John Kennedy of Lochboisdale Hotel, is not only an excellent seatrout fly which takes salmon but has also a growing reputation as a bob fly for brown trout, especially in Lewis.
Hook: 10-6
Tag: Two turns flat silver
Tail: Scarlet wool over yellow (or Glo-Brite floss 4 and 10)
Body: Black seal's fur
Rib: Medium oval silver
Body hackles: Scarlet and black cock, wound together
Collar hackle: Black hen.
Leven Spider, invented by Ian Macdonald of Heriot's FP, has now

many variations. I use it on the tail, tied on a size 14 LS hook, using red tying thread, with a lime-green fluorescent wool tail, gold mylar body, black hen hackle and a red varnished head. It is also effective as a dropper (12 or 14 short shank) and is an excellent single fly (14) on a long, fine leader when the wind goes in the evening and fish are moving.

Maclean's Red Zulu is native born, originated by John M Maclean of Stornoway back in 1982 as a variation of the Blue Zulu and developed over the years, with extensive field testing by himself and friends, until its final version was made public in 1993. Like the Blue Zulu, it takes all our game fish. The dressing is:

Hook: Kamasan LS 12-8
Thread: Black
Rib: Oval silver
Body: Fluorescent red Antron wool
Body hackle: Palmered black cock
Collar hackle: Blue cock (as Blue Zulu).

The Solicitor, the first of three great flies created by Iain MacGregor Christie of Skye, is that rarity, a truly great middle dropper which usually outfishes the other flies on better positions on the leader.

Hook: (I seem always to use a size 12)
Tail: Small bunch of hot orange cock hackles
Rib: Fine oval gold
Body: Gold lurex
Body hackle: Ginger cock, stripped of one side
Collar hackle: Furnace.

Two of his other flies are also of the highest class.

Charlie Maclean is a bob fly and a great mover of fish.
Hook: According to conditions
Tail: Short tuft of orange fluorescent wool
Tag: Two turns of flat silver in front of tail
Rear hackle: A few turns of white cock tied to slope back
Rib: Oval silver through body hackle
Body hackle: Furnace cock, doubled
Collar hackle: Two or three turns white cock, sloping back

All the hackles should be tied long. Wee Peter is a modification of the Peter Ross — a gilding of the lily which works well. It is an excellent high summer trout fly, size 12.

Tail: Sparse bunch of hot orange or scarlet cock
Body: Underbody of flat silver left to show as rear two-thirds.
  Two turns scarlet fluorescent wool over front third
Collar hackle: Two or three turns black hen.

Mini-Muddlers (sizes 12-10) can be fished on bob or tail in all their different dressings. I find a single size 12 Butcher type works well in an evening calm, twitched gently on an intermediate line.

Hoppers in all their varieties fish well all season and deserve to be experimented with fished dry, sub-surface or wet.

Salmon Flies

These are traditionally known as "salmon flies", but it should be emphasised again that salmon are caught here on both traditional trout flies and on others not normally associated with salmon fishing. The flies listed here all work on rivers as well as lochs. The usual loch leader has a double or even a small treble on the tail and a single, often bushy, bob fly. However, some swear by three flies as giving a better balance to the leader, but where weed is about this can be a hazard.

Stoat's Tail is always reliable, as is the Silver Stoat's Tail. My particular favourite is this Silver version but with a rich blue hackle. Sweep on the tail and Thunder and Lightning on the bob was the cast recommended to me many years ago by John Maciver, Head Keeper at Soval Estate, and the combination has proved its worth on many occasions. Jock Scott, Silver Doctor, Silver Wilkinson, Mar Lodge, Logie, Blue Charm, etc in the old feather-winged style were once essentials and, often tied as hairwings, still take fish. Particularly good is Watson's Fancy, late in the season. Arthur Ransome's Blue Elver (miniaturised by the old Grimersta gillies) still works well as a bob fly, especially in a big wave, though now seriously challenged by the Muddler. Hairy Mary is very dependable, and Kenny's Killer works well in early and mid-season. Green Highlander, once very popular here, has made something of a comeback in its hairwing dressing.

Black Brahan gave me my first Lewis salmon, and the Munro Killer can be as good on lochs as it is on the Spey.

Late in the season flies with some yellow in them, such as the Garry Dog and Tosh, or a black-and- yellow tube fly in rivers, are often effective.

Spring salmon are now very rare, and so summer fly sizes are based on eight as a standard, but vary sizes to suit the conditions or your whims. Although shock tactics using a large fly more suited to spring fishing on the Tay are sometimes successful, size 10 or 8 doubles, standard or low water, on the tail and something bushy on the bob will work more often. In difficult conditions of little wind and low water very small flies down to trout 12s can be very successful, but adjust your leader thickness accordingly.

The Hairwing Blue Charm and its variation, the Flashing Charmer (about four strands of Pearl Lureflash mixed into the wing), are reliable flies which also look good to the angler.

Miscellaneous

Dry Flies and Emergers:
These are little used because wild brown trout are usually well scat-

tered over the loch and have to be prospected for. Nevertheless, the dry fly can work even when no fish are rising, floated in a cross breeze from the bank or from a boat in low winds. Greenwell's Glory and the Knotted Midge can work well. Experiment.

Nymphs, Pupae, Buzzers and the like:
Such flies from the reservoirs of the Lowlands and the South are all useful at times. A small leaded nymph works well in calm conditions in the evening. Again, much more experimenting remains to be done.

Clyde Style Flies:
These can be deadly in a low wave, or fished singly in a calm rather like a nymph, especially the Hen Blackie, Murray's Bluebottle Spider, Murray's Firefly and Cran Swallow, usually on size 14 hooks.

Dapping Flies:
Dapping is a technique slowly gaining favour in the Isles, but much experimenting remains to be done. The flies are legion and defy classification!

BIBLIOGRAPHY

Adamson W A : Lake and Loch Fishing for Salmon and Sea Trout (A & C Black, 1961)
Bickerdyke John : Days in Thule, With Rod, Gun and Camera (Constable & Co, London, 1894)
Boyd J M & Boyd I C : The Hebrides, A Natural History (Collins, The New Naturalist Library, 1990)
Braithwaite Cecil : Fishing Vignettes (Home Words 1923?)
Fishing Here and There (Home Words 1932?)
Happy Days with Rod, Gun and Bat (Home Words 1946?)
Bridgett R C : Loch Fishing in Theory and Practice (Herbert Jenkins, 1924)
Sea Trout Fishing (Herbert Jenkins, 1929) — A useful chapter on fishing in Harris.
Buckland John and Oglesby Arthur : A Guide to Salmon Flies (Crowood Press, 1990)
Chrystal Major R A : Angling at Lochboisdale (Witherby, 1939)
Clarke Brian: The Pursuit of Stillwater Trout (A & C Black, 1975)
Cunningham Peter : A Hebridean Naturalist (Acair, Stornoway, 1979)
Birds of The Outer Hebrides, A Guide to their Status and Distribution (The Melven Press, Perth, 1983, Revised edition 1990)
Falkus Hugh : Sea Trout Fishing (Witherby, 1975, Second Revised Edition)
Salmon Fishing (Witherby, 1984)
Lake, Loch & Reservoir Trout Fishing: Malcolm Greenhalgh (A&C Black 1987)
Harris Graeme and Morgan Moc : Successful Sea Trout Angling (Blandford, 1989)
Hely-Hutchinson Rev George Henry : Reminiscences of The Lews, Twenty Years of Wild Sport in The Hebrides (Bickers & Son, London, 1873)
Henzell H P : The Art and Craft of Loch Fishing (Philip Allan 1937)
Fishing for Seatrout (A & C Black, 1949)
Kennedy John : 70 Lochs, A Guide to Trout fishing in South Uist (Uist Community Press, Balivanich)
Malcolm Greenhalgh: Lake, Loch & Reservoir Trout Fishing (A. & C. Black, 1987)
McLaren Charles C : The Art of Sea Trout Fishing (Oliver & Boyd, 1963 , Revised Unwin Hyman, 1989)
Macleod Norman : Trout Fishing in Lewis (Essprint, Stornoway, 1977, 1985. Completely revised and enlarged by Roddy J Macleod and Eddie Young, 1993)
Malone E J . Irish Trout and Salmon Flies (Colin Smythe, 1984)
Moore T C Kingsmill : A Man May Fish (Colin Smythe, 1960, Revised 1979)
Morgan Moc : Fly Patterns for the Rivers and Lakes of Wales (Gomer Press, 1984)
Newall Captain J T : Scottish Moors and Indian Jungles (Hurst & Blackett, London, 1889)
Oatts Colonel H A : Loch Trout (Herbert Jenkins, 1958)
Peel C V A : Wild Sport in the Outer Hebrides (F E Robinson, London, 1901)
Ransome Arthur: Rod and Line (Cape, 1929)
Mainly About Fishing (A & C Black, 1959)

Reid John : Clyde Style Flies (David and Charles, 1971)
Scott Jock : Sea Trout Fishing (Lonsdale Library, Sealey Service, 1969)
Spencer Sydney : The Art of Lake Fishing with sunk fly (Witherby, 1934)
Salmon and Sea Trout in Wild Places (Witherby 1968), Newly from the Sea (Witherby, 1969), Ways of Fishing (Witherby, 1972),94 Game Fishing Tactics (Witherby, 1974)
Spencer's books are difficult to obtain. There is a useful compilation of selected extracts by Jeremy Lucas, Fishing the Wilder Shores (Witherby, 1991)
Stewart Tom : 200 Popular Flies (Ernest Benn, 1982)
Stewart W C : The Practical Angler (A & C Black, 1857)
Although Stewart is more famous for his advocacy of the upstream wet fly, his book contains an interesting and very sensible chapter on loch fishing.
Stuart Hamish : The Book of the Sea Trout: with some chapters on Salmon (Martin Secker, 1917)
Townsend Douglas C : Fly Tying with Harold Howorth (A & C Black, 1980)
Waltham James : Sea Trout Flies (A & C Black, 1988)